Words of the Dead Chief

✳

CLASSICS OF IRISH HISTORY
General Editor: Tom Garvin

Some recent titles
Original publication dates of reprinted titles are given in brackets

941.58

0 0 NOV 2009

NA

DCPL0000138114

Items should be returned on or before the last date
shown below. Items not already requested by other
borrowers may be renewed in person, in writing or by
telephone. To re~   ~~ ~uote the number on the
barco~

Words of the Dead Chief

Being Extracts from the Public
Speeches and Other Pronouncements of
Charles Stewart Parnell from the Beginning
to the Close of his Remarkable Life

:✦.

CHARLES STEWART PARNELL

compiled by Jennie Wyse-Power
with an introduction by Anna Parnell
edited by Donal McCartney and Pauric Travers

UNIVERSITY COLLEGE DUBLIN PRESS
Preas Choláiste Ollscoile Bhaile Átha Cliath

First published in Dublin by Sealy, Bryers and Walker, 1892
This edition published by University College Dublin Press, 2009
New Introduction and notes © Donal McCartney and Pauric Travers, 2009
Compilation of speeches © the Estate of Jennie Wyse-Power, 2009

ISBN 978-1-906359-42-3
ISSN 1393-6883

University College Dublin Press
Newman House, 86 St Stephen's Green
Dublin 2, Ireland
www.ucdpress.ie

Cataloguing in Publication data available
from the British Library

Typeset in Ehrhardt by Elaine Burberry
Text design by Lyn Davies, Frome, Somerset, England
Printed in England on acid-free paper by
Antony Rowe, Chippenham, Wilts.

CONTENTS

ACKNOWLEDGEMENTS

The editors wish to thank Mr Leslie Armstrong of Rathdrum, Co. Wicklow for making available to us his copy of the original *Words of the Dead Chief.*

They also thank the Committee of the Parnell Society for its support.

INTRODUCTION TO NEW EDITION
Donal McCartney and Pauric Travers

Words of the Dead Chief is a collection of extracts from the speeches of Charles Stewart Parnell. Many of Parnell's best-known speeches are included. Written shortly after his death, the book is dedicated 'To the Memory of the Dead'. There is an unmistakeable political even propagandist dimension to the publication. It is written for a nationalist audience and particularly for the followers of Parnell. In her preface, Jennie Wyse-Power explains that the purpose of her 'humble memento' was to keep the principles that Parnell enunciated before the minds of Irish nationalists 'for whom they should be a rule of political faith and conduct'. She aimed 'to select such passages as were most characteristic of himself [Parnell], of greatest significance in their bearing upon questions of practical politics, and of most vital importance for Irish nationalists to study, to remember, and to take for guidance'. As such, *Words of the Dead Chief* is itself an important text from a critical period in Irish nationalist politics and history. It is much else besides.

Wyse-Power's collection was an immediate bestseller. It was easily accessible to a general audience and proved highly influential. However, it quickly went out of print. Copies are now exceedingly rare, even in major libraries. Wyse-Power anticipated that, in time, a 'more comprehensive volume of Mr Parnell's speeches will be prepared by some person better qualified for the task than I am'. However, no such collection has yet been published. Despite its obvious limitations, *Words of the Dead Chief* remains an invaluable source and hence its republication. Parnell left remarkably little in the way of letters, diaries or published works. Historians are dependent to an unusually large extent on his speeches as signposts to the development his political thought.

Jane Wyse-Power (*née* O'Toole) was a significant figure in her own right as a nationalist and feminist. While there is a useful biography by Marie O'Neill, the republication of *Words of the Dead Chief* should contribute to a fuller rehabilitation of a significant figure in the history of Irish women.[1] Born in 1858 in Baltinglass, west Wicklow, approximately 60 kilometres from Avondale, the Parnell ancestral home, she was the youngest of seven children of Edward O'Toole, provision dealer, and his wife, Mary Norton. When she was a very young child, the family moved to Dublin and set up shop in Cuffe Street and later Johnson Place. Jennie was educated at a local convent school. Politically, the O'Toole family sympathies were strongly nationalist and the family home over the shop became a meeting place for the Fenians and a centre of political activity. Jennie's public initiation into political activism came through the Land League campaign and, in particular, the Ladies' Land League, which she joined in 1881, quickly becoming a member of the executive and playing a prominent role in its organisation nationally

The Ladies' Land League was a significant element in the politicisation of many Irish women. Founded initially as a fund-raising organisation in the United States by Fanny Parnell, it was established in Ireland by Anna Parnell and assumed a more central role after the imprisonment of the male leaders of the Land League in October 1881. The activities of the Ladies' League generated hostility and criticism from some who disliked its radicalism and others who were uncomfortable with the prominence of women in the public sphere. When the male leaders were released in May 1882, the Ladies' League was suppressed and the wider nationalist movement took a new direction under the leadership of Charles Stewart Parnell.

Despite the inevitable disillusionment at what many saw as betrayal of the Ladies' League by the male leadership, Jennie continued to support Parnell and was active in his cause during the Split. In 1883, Jennie married John Wyse-Power, a journalist, member of the Irish Republican Brotherhood and one of the founders of the Gaelic Athletic Association (GAA). They had four children, three girls and a boy, born five months after the death of Parnell and christened Charles Stewart Wyse-Power in his honour.[2] She was a prominent member of the Parnell Leadership Committee, and when Parnell died she and her husband were closely involved in the organisation of his funeral. She became treasurer of the women's committee that looked after Parnell's grave at Glasnevin and participated annually in the Ivy Day commemorations.

Like many of her generation, Wyse-Power's political outlook was significantly affected by the Parnellite Split. The Parnellite virtues which she sought to illustrate in her choice of extracts from his speeches – self-reliance and independence – were consistently manifest in her own political career. She joined the Gaelic League in 1893 and, in 1899, established the Irish Farm Produce Company in Henry Street, with a restaurant attached. The family home above the shop, like her parent's home, became a nationalist meeting place – the 1916 proclamation was signed there. She was an active supporter of the cause of women's suffrage and radical nationalism, being a member of the Irishwomen's Suffrage and Local Government Association and the Irish Women's Franchise League and, in 1900, a founder member of Inghinidhe na hÉireann. In 1905, she co-founded the National Council which later became Sinn Féin and she was a long-time member of its executive. She was an active member of Cumann na mBan (established in 1914), and supported the Easter rebellion. After the rising, she once again became a member of the executive and served as Treasurer of Sinn Féin and as a judge in the Sinn Féin courts. She was elected Poor Law Guardian in Dublin South in 1903 and member of Dublin Corporation in 1920. Surprisingly perhaps, she supported the Treaty in 1921, joined Cumann na nGaedheal and became a member of Seanad Éireann. However, she became disillusioned with the failure to make progress on ending partition and became an independent in 1925. Attracted by its advocacy of self-sufficiency, she later joined Fianna Fáil. With the abolition of the Senate in 1936, her active political life came to an end but she continued to be a strong supporter of woman's rights. She died in 1941 and is buried in Glasnevin cemetery, beside her husband who predeceased her, and not far from the 'Dead Chief'.

Jennie Wyse-Power's involvement in the Ladies' Land League brought her into close contact with Anna Parnell.[3] While they came from very different backgrounds, they shared Wicklow and Dublin roots and both were articulate, independent and outspoken. They worked together closely at the helm of the Ladies' League and maintained a friendship afterwards. Unlike Wyse-Power, Anna Parnell largely withdrew from public life after 1882 and only intermittently emerged thereafter. The suppression of the Ladies' League resulted in a deep division between Anna and her brother Charles; Wyse-Power sought to maintain a loyalty to both. Anna Parnell's agreement to write an introduction to the *Words of the Dead Chief* reflects the success of that endeavour and throws some light on her relationship with her brother. Katharine O'Shea claimed that Anna never forgave her brother for his betrayal of the Ladies' Land League and never spoke to him again. William O'Brien corroborates this, although he is not necessarily a reliable witness. When Tim Healy repeated the allegation in 1891, Anna publicly denied it.[4] It would appear that her distaste for her brother's critics and her own deeply held belief in the need for an independent, self-reliant nationalist movement outweighed her lingering annoyance at the events of 1882.

Anna Parnell's introduction is characteristically blunt and forceful and confines itself largely to political principles and ideology. Reflecting the context in which it is written, it challenges two 'bogies' – Irish disunion and English disapprobation and offers in their stead the ideal of independence and self-reliance. English politicians from Pitt to Gladstone are placed in the dock alongside Irish place-seekers who sacrifice principle, honour, justice and self-respect at the shrine of expediency. Anna Parnell was convinced that progress towards that ideal would take many years and would require a major upheaval. Her chosen epigraph –'they are slaves who dare not be/ in the right with two or three'[5] – emphasises her fundamental belief that the majority had no right to betray the wider national ideal, and echoes debates within the nationalist movement a generation later. Her belief that the majority had no right to be wrong is probably derived from J. S. Mill's doctrine of 'the tyranny of the majority' – Anna was an intellectual and a friend of Mill's stepdaughter, Helen Taylor.

One might have expected some personal intimate family reflections or vignettes but, as with her later account of the Land League, *The Tale of a Great Sham* (Dublin, 1986), Anna Parnell insisted in sublimating the personal. There is, however, an unmistakeable tone of bitterness at those who lead a 'comrade' into an ambush by 'false professions and promises, and insincere solicitations, then to desert him there, to hand him over to his enemy, and to help that enemy to destroy him'. [6] Her choice of the word 'comrade' rather than leader or chief is revealing – Anna Parnell did not subscribe to the cult of leadership, possibly following Henry Buckle's critique of Carlyle's 'hero' theory. She made no exception in the case of her brother. In her analysis of the limitations of Home Rule, she is implicitly highly critical of his earlier acceptance of Gladstone's limited proposal.

A facsimile of a portion of Parnell's famous 'Manifesto to the Irish People' is also included in *Words of the Dead Chief*. The facsimile (see p. 141) reproduces page 2 of Parnell's original draft. This controversial document was perhaps the longest ever penned by him. Parnell wrote it in the home of Dr J. G. Fitzgerald in Eccleston Street, Chester Square from noon to night on Friday 28 November 1890. Fitzgerald was MP for Longford South (1888–92), and remained loyal to his leader throughout the Split. When the draft was finished, Parnell sent for a few of his loyal friends (including the Redmonds and J. J. O'Kelly) and also for the Party's vice-chairman, Justin McCarthy. He read it to them and then gave it to a journalist of the *Freeman's Journal* for publication. The published version appeared in the *Freeman's Journal*, 29 November 1890, and is given in F. S. L. Lyons, *The Fall of Parnell*.[7] Nine foolscap pages (about half of Parnell's manuscript) have survived, and were presented by Dr Fitzgerald to Eamon de Valera in July 1921. These pages are now in the National Library of Ireland.[8] Page 2 of the manuscript which is reproduced in *Words of the Dead Chief* (1892) was probably loaned to Wyse-Power by her fellow Parnellite, Dr Fitzgerald. A year later an article by Fitzgerald himself in the *Irish Weekly Independent*, 6 October 1893, also carried a reproduction of the same page. What is remarkable about the manuscript are how few corrections Parnell made to his draft.

*   *   *

We know almost nothing beyond what we can surmise about Jennie Wyse-Power's *modus operandi* in researching and locating relevant speeches by Parnell and selecting extracts for inclusion in her book. Parnell did not retain collections of his own speeches or notes and it would appear that Wyse-Power worked mainly from newspaper reports, and particularly *The Nation*. Parnell's political speeches fall into three main categories: election or campaign speeches in Ireland and England, speeches in the United States, and speeches in the House of Commons.[9] The first and to a lesser extent the second of these categories is well represented in Wyse-Power's collection but not the third. Abstracts from only seven statements are given from his mission to America where between 2 January and 11 March 1880 Parnell spoke in 62 different cities. Yet brief as all these abstracts are, they convey something of his principles and force of character.

Heavily pregnant while she was doing her research, Jennie had little scope for visits to libraries and archives in Britain and the United States so she relied predominantly on Irish nationalist newspapers. Presumably John Wyse-Power's background as a journalist was helpful – he was a political journalist and leader writer for the *Freeman's Journal* until shortly before Parnell's death but moved to the Parnellite *Irish Independent* when Edward Gray Junior, the owner of the *Freeman*, reversed that paper's position and opposed Parnell.[10] Given the constraints, the collection is broadly representative.

Clearly all Parnell's speeches could not be included; inevitably, there are some glaring omissions. One of Parnell's most famous speeches is excluded – that at Westport on 8 June 1879 when he exhorted the tenant farmers: 'You must show the landlords that you intend to hold a firm grip on your homesteads and lands. You must not allow yourselves to be dispossessed as your fathers were dispossessed in 1847.' What he said at Westport was repeated, however, in much the same phrases at Limerick on 31 August 1879 and is included below under than date.

While an extract from Parnell's address to Congress during his American visit in 1880 is included, his controversial speech at Cincinnati on 20 February, when he reportedly referred to breaking the last link with Britain, is not. The speech is a key text; its omission here is significant. The question of what Parnell did or did not say continues to be debated by historians.[11] In 1886, when the first Home Rule bill was being introduced, the speech was resurrected to show that Parnell's new found moderation was a sham and it was again produced in 1889 at the Special Commission hearings to show a connection between Parnell and Fenianism. Parnell told the Special Commission that it was most improbable that he had used the words referred to and produced a report of his speech from *the Cincinnati Daily Gazette* which did not include the remarks; nor did they appear in the report published by the *Cincinnati Journal*. However, they did appear in the *Cincinnati Commercial Gazette* and later in the *Irish World*.[12] Barry O'Brien later concluded that, at Cincinnati, Parnell spoke from the heart and that the more radical version of the Cincinnati speech represented his true position.

Parnell's remarkable speech on the second reading of the Home Rule bill in June 1886 is another unfortunate omission. Historians are divided on whether the speech is best interpreted as an uncompromising statement of an irredentist position or a subtle and visionary manifesto for a pluralist Ireland.[13] Wyse-Power includes an extract from a related Parnell speech in Belfast in May 1891, but omits the passages that have attracted most interest from historians – those which relate to the need for conciliation of the Protestant minority – in favour of those emphasising self-reliance and the need for an independent Irish Party.[14]

Parnell, according to F. S. L. Lyons, was a 'wretched speaker'.[15] This negative judgement echoes the verdict of many of Parnell's contemporaries and later historians. A. M. Sullivan who was present at Parnell's debut on the hustings in 1874 as the prospective candidate for County Dublin concluded that he would be known as 'single speech Parnell';[16] J. G. Swift MacNeill recalled that on that occasion Parnell could 'only say a few disjointed words',[17] while

O'Connor Power 'listened to him with pain while he was on his legs' and 'felt immensely relieved when he sat down.'[18] R. Barry O'Brien, Parnell's earliest biographer, concluded that 'Parnell disliked speechifying . . . and had not the least ambition to become a great public speaker'.[19] However, the continued currency of such speeches as 'Hold a firm grip on your homesteads' (Westport, 1879) and 'No man has the right to set the boundary to the march of the nation' (Cork, 1885), which have entered the popular consciousness, give reason for pause before discounting too easily his powers of political communication. It is undeniable that Parnell's early efforts as an orator were poor and that he was never a natural orator; however, he adjusted to the demands of the hustings and developed a distinctive and powerful style as a public speaker that was all the more effective for being different.

One contemporary journalist, who observed Parnell's rapid ascent to the forefront of Irish politics, considered that his speeches were always clear and to the point but that he had hardly any of the attributes of a popular leader as he was 'singularly unimpassioned as an orator' and had an English accent, a 'serious disqualification for an Irish patriot'.[20] Such negative comments on Parnell's oratory partly reflect a conventional public taste for a florid, eighteenth-century style which survived in Ireland longer than elsewhere. Parnell did not fit that mould: only occasionally did he resort to literary reference, metaphor, redundant adjectives, humour or playfulness of language, but he could speak with devastating directness.

Parnell was more a man of action than words. He once confided to Andrew Kettle, later to be his candidate in the Carlow by-election in 1891, that he was not 'gifted with the power of expression of some other men'. Kettle reassured him that 'the orators use too many adjectives. You are going to found a talking school of your own with ideas instead of words.'[21] During the Carlow election, Parnell told an audience in Bagnalstown that he had 'never pretended in my public life to any eloquence or what is called oratorical power. I have always endeavoured to be a practical man and a practical statesman'.[22] This is both an honest self-assessment and a revealing insight into Parnell's self-conscious creation of a distinctive persona and a related style of public speaking.

In November 1878, William O'Brien who observed a speech by Parnell in Tralee recalled that despite a difficult audience Parnell fired them all before he sat down.[23] Gladstone said that Parnell had the rarest of qualities in a speaker – measure, while John Morley considered him 'a consummate swordsman' with 'a supple and trenchant blade'.[24] Morley who heard Parnell's speech in the House of Commons on the second reading of the first Home Rule bill considered that it was one of his most masterly speeches and that Parnell possessed the secret of Demosthenic oratory.[25] Demosthenes who led the struggle of the Athenians to maintain their freedom against Philip of Macedonia posed the rhetorical question at his trial in 330 BC: In what circumstances, then, ought a statesman and an orator to be vehement? and answered: when the state is in jeopardy. It is precisely at the moments of greatest importance for the nation that Parnell's speeches rise from the mundane to the memorable.[26] Coincidently, in a speech at Navan in March 1891 dealing with the fateful Committee Room 15 debates in the House of Commons when he was deposed, Parnell invokes 'the eloquence of Demosthenes and the ability of Cicero' while ostensibly denying that he possessed such skills.

Parnell's posture while speaking publicly was unconventional – he stood stiffly with his arms folded loosely in front of him or sometimes behind his back. He spoke in a low voice, slowly and distinctly; he rarely raised his voice or gestured or gesticulated. He had an aversion to shouting.[27] He often gave the impression of indifference to an audience which one critic suggested made him 'meagre' in his style'.[28] One observer commented that what struck him most about Parnell was his silence: 'One was not accustomed to it. All Irish agitators talked. He didn't.'[29] In the bitter struggle that followed the Split, Parnell had little option but to become more communicative. A neutral spectator at Parnell's Ulster Hall speech in Belfast, in May 1891, who considered that the speech was 'important, clear, forcible, statesmanlike' recalled that he began slowly and calmly and then gradually became more animated and 'even warm, but on the whole his tone was reserved, cool and forcible, not a point failing to be pressed home . . . He discussed with active calmness, moving about freely on the platform, usually in his favourite attitude, with arms folded'.[30]

Parnell disliked impromptu speaking but could be extremely effective as is illustrated by an unscheduled speech at Bagnalstown during the Carlow election in 1891 (not included by Wyse-Power). Speaking from the window of Ward's Hotel, Parnell disclaimed eloquence and oratorical prowess but proceeded to display it in abundance. He reminded his audience of the difference between words and deeds, oratory and action, leadership and subservience and then dismissed his critics to lesser roles. A trenchant blade is evident: he used a military metaphor of armies, generals and foot-soldiers to assert his own leadership and diminish Tim Healy's role before raising the eyes of his audience to higher things, invoking his favourite biblical image from the period of the Split – the wilderness in which they sojourned and the promised land to which he was about to lead his countrymen:

I have always endeavoured to find out as many eloquent Irishmen as possible to supply my own deficiencies in this respect, because my view of every man is that he is capable of some good if you keep him to the work for which he is best qualified. That was my view with reference to Tim Healy when I first brought him out . . . Every general's duty is to select the men best fitted for the different branches of the service. Some men are good for cavalry, no use for artillery, and some good as skirmishers, and so we got together a fine Irish army in Westminster until the time came when two or three or four of the skirmishers thought they ought to become generals (groans and laughter) . . . I ask you to permit me having led you so far through the wilderness, until we are in sight of the promised land, until we are almost entering within the gates – not to thrust me back but to allow me to enter these gates with you (cheers). And when we have obtained for Ireland the right to make laws on Irish soil, and the right to enforce these laws when they are made, when we have obtained the power for our people to secure the prosperity, freedom and liberty of all classes of Irishmen and Irishwomen, then, fellow-countrymen, if you like, you will be able to select a man in my place to watch and guide the interests of our nation and to help our country take her legitimate place amongst the nations of the world.[31]

This speech demonstrates the need not to take the words uttered at face value. Notwithstanding his reputation for directness and plain speaking, Parnell understood the creative value of ambiguity and the necessity to convey different messages to different constituencies even in the same speech.[32] Hence, for example, the careful balance of the apparent *carte blanche* in his rousing '*ne plus ultra*' speech in Cork in January 1885, with the caveat that for the moment all that was on the menu was the very limited option of the restoration of Grattan's parliament.[33] The Cork formula – a combination of rhetorical flourish with less conspicuous reservation – was most effectively used during the land war 1879–81 and after the Split, although in the latter case the reservation was understandably less conspicuous.

This raises the related questions of audience, context and dissemination. Parnell was well aware that audiences varied and had different needs: Irish audiences, he famously observed, needed to be encouraged and lifted up because 'they are oppressed and beaten down'. On the other hand, he felt Irish-American audiences, 'require to have cold water thrown upon them'.[34] Wyse-Power provides little background or context for individual speeches and the inclusion of many short extracts makes deeper analysis more difficult. Much of the flavour and impact of the speeches are lost when detached from the particular context – whether that context be an enthusiastic gathering of tenant farmers or a rowdy and hostile election meeting. However, many of Parnell's speeches do suit this approach. A characteristic feature is that while they were carefully constructed in terms of balance, they tend to contain accessible and memorable slogans. Stirring rhetoric has less enduring impact on an audience than a catchy phrase constantly repeated. Parnell grasped early the value of the sound bite and the need to ensure dissemination of the message. He took considerable care to facilitate journalists at meetings – for instance, always being accompanied by a journalist on election campaigns.[35]

In the Carlow election, Parnell needed to assert his leadership while winning or regaining the confidence of the local electorate. Notwithstanding his reputation for remoteness and stiffness, he self-consciously sought to establish a link with his audience, personalising his remarks, flattering his listeners, stressing the close affinity between Wicklow and Carlow, often citing history – notwithstanding his reputation to the contrary – and occasionally resorting to humour.[36] In one instance when there was a threat that the meeting would be disrupted by 'the mountainy men', he responded humorously, 'I am not afraid of the mountainy men (cheers), . . . I am a "goat sucker" myself, and the Wicklow mountains and the Carlow mountains that reared Holt and Dwyer are not going to send men to ask Irishmen to bend the knee to English dictation (cheers)'.[37]

Parnell demonstrated great skill and eloquence in a number of instances in Carlow, any one of which might rate a place in a compendium of great Irish speeches. His address rallying his forces after the declaration of the poll is arguably one of his finest. Parnell

responded to his defeat prophetically with great dignity and eloquence. Wyse-Power only includes a short extract which loses much
of the force of a powerful address: [38]

> Now my friends our army is the Old Guard (cheers). It is composed of
> the same materials which Napoleon called upon at Waterloo (cheers), the
> men who handed down to their children the traditions of the chivalry of
> France, and who were rewarded for their patriotism and their bravery by
> the freedom of their beloved land (cheers) . . . these are the feelings,
> which actuate our supporters and their friends (cheers). They fight for
> Ireland, they do not fight for themselves (cheers). They live not only for
> today – they have inherited the traditions of those who bled and died in
> this great country, and they look to the future confident that those who
> now follow the miserable cries which have been sought to be substituted
> in this contest for the call of patriotism will soon see, and will soon have
> to seek shelter behind the invincible phalanx which the patriotism of
> Carlow presents today and which the patriotism of Ireland will present
> tomorrow (loud cheers); for
>
> > Freedom's battle once begun –
> > Bequeathed by bleeding sire to son –
> > Though baffled oft' is always won. [39]

Notes to Introduction

1 *Irish Independent*, 6, 7, 8 Jan. 1941; Marie O'Neill, *From Parnell to De Valera: A
Biography of Jennie Wyse Power, 1858–1941* (Dublin, 1991). The biographical details
cited above are taken mainly from O'Neill and from Mary Cullen's entry, 'Power,
Jane Wyse (1858–1941)', *Oxford Dictionary of National Biography* (Oxford, 2004).
2 Charles Stewart Wyse-Power later became a nationalist and was a distinguished jurist and circuit court judge on the western circuit. *Irish Independent*,
20 June 1950.

3   For Anna Parnell and the Ladies' Land League, see P. Travers, '"No turning back": Anna Parnell, identity, memory and gender', in D. McCartney and P. Travers, *The Ivy Leaf: The Parnells Remembered* (Dublin, 2006), pp 124–39.

4   Katharine O'Shea, *Charles Stewart Parnell: His Love Story and Political Life* (London, 1914), I, p. 261; William O'Brien, *Evening Memories* (London, 1920), p. 188; William O'Brien, *Recollections* (London, 1905), p.463; *National Press*, 27 Mar. 1891; *Irish Times*, 13 Oct. 1891.

5   This is an adaptation of a couplet in Lowell's abolitionist poem 'On freedom' which reads: 'He's a slave who fears to be . . .'.

6   Anna Parnell's tone and language is reminiscent of James Joyce's Parnell. Coincidently the Wyse-Powers were family friends of the Joyces; Jennie makes a fleeting appearance in *Ulysses* as Mrs John Wyse Nolan.

7   F. S. L. Lyons, *The Fall of Parnell* (London, 1960), pp. 320–6.

8   National Library of Ireland, MS 21,933.

9   R. Barry O'Brien, *The Life of Charles Stewart Parnell* (London, 1898) I, p. 85. On Parnell's American speeches, see Donal McCartney, 'Parnell and the American connection', in McCartney and Travers (eds), *The Ivy Leaf*, pp. 38–55.

10 O'Neill, *Jennie Wyse Power*, p. 41.

11 Lyons, *Parnell*, pp. 111–13; Barry O'Brien, *Parnell*, I, p.206.

12 M. V. Hazel, 'First link: Parnell's American tour, 1880', *Éire–Ireland* XV: 1 (1980), 17–18; *Special Commission Act, 1888. Proceedings and Evidence* (London 1889) pp. 7, 22–3, 110–17, 282.

13 For an extract from the speech and the differing interpretations, see P. Travers, 'Parnell and the Ulster question' in D. McCartney (ed.), *Parnell: The Politics of Power* (Dublin, 1991), pp. 67–8.

14 *Northern Whig*, 23 May 1891; Paul Bew, *Parnell* (Dublin, 1980), pp. 128–9.

15 F. S. L. Lyons, *Charles Stewart Parnell* (Fontana, 1977), p. 57.

16 Barry O'Brien, *Parnell*, I, p. 74.

17 J. G. Swift MacNeill, *What I have Seen and Heard* (London 1925), pp. 145–6.

18 Barry O'Brien, *Parnell*, I, pp. 74–5.

19 Ibid., pp. 86–7.

20 Richard Pigott, *Personal Recollections of an Irish National Journalist* (Dublin, 1882 and Cork, 1979), p. 349.

21 *Material for Victory: The Memoirs of Andrew J. Kettle*, ed. Laurence J. Kettle. (Dublin, 1958), p. 33.

22 *Freeman's Journal*, 6 July 1891. On the Carlow election, see P. Travers, 'Calling the kettle black: Parnell, oratory and invective', *Carloviana*: Journal of the Carlow Historical and Archaeological Society, no. 57 (Dec. 2008).

23 Michael MacDonagh, *The Life of William O'Brien* (London, 1928), p. 50.

24 John Morley, *Recollections* (London, 1917), I, p. 241; John Morley, *The Life of William Ewart Gladstone* (London, 1903), III, pp. 313, 376–7, 448, 450–1; Swift MacNeill, *Seen and Heard*, pp. 145–6; House of Commons Debates, CCLXXVI, 482.

25 Morley, *Gladstone*, III, pp. 313, 337.

26 Brian MacArthur, *The Penguin Book of Historic Speeches* (London 1996), pp. 71–3.

27 John Howard Parnell, *Charles Stewart Parnell: A Memoir* (London, 1916), p. 175.

28 Morley, *Gladstone*, III, p. 399.

29 Barry O'Brien, *Parnell*, p. 137.

30 *Witness*, 29 May 1891 quoted in Bew, *Parnell*, p. 128.

31 *Freeman's Journal*, 6 July 1891.

32 For an elaboration on these issues of text and context in the case of Parnell's speeches, see Travers, 'Reading between the lines: the political speeches of Charles Stewart Parnell', in McCartney and Travers (eds), *The Ivy Leaf*, pp. 56–68.

33 Oliver MacDonagh, *States of Mind: A Study of Anglo-Irish Conflict, 1780–1980* (London, 1983), pp. 59–61.

34 Michael Davitt, *The Fall of Feudalism in Ireland* (London, 1904) p. 205.

35 James Loughlin, 'Constructing the political spectacle: Parnell, the press and national leadership, 1879–1886', in Boyce and O'Day, *Parnell in Perspective*, p. 225.

36 *Freeman's Journal*, 2 July 1891.

37 Ibid., 30 June 1891.

38 Ibid., 8 July 1881.

39 Ibid., 9 July 1891. These lines from Byron were quoted also by John Mitchel in his *Jail Journal* under the date 1 January 1850.

Note on the Text

The text of *Words of the Dead Chief* has been typeset from the original Sealy, Bryers & Walker edition published in Dublin in 1892. It is likely that most of the pieces selected by Jennie Wyse-Power were taken from newspaper reports. Parnell's words are mostly presented in direct quotations from his speeches, but in some cases these are given in reported speech, which might confusingly appear at first sight to be quotations from direct speech as they are displayed in quotation marks. The layout of the extracts reproduced in this book is close to that of the original; any additions we have made are given in square brackets. Jennie Wyse-Power added brief contextual explanations at the beginning of some of the speeches. These and any additions within the speeches that we suspect were made by her, and which were printed in square brackets in the original book, are shown here inside curly brackets{ }. Some comments within the extracts were not, however, printed in square brackets in the original text. These may have been included in the previously published pieces Wyse-Power selected or they may have been further additions by her; we have left these untouched. Comments in parentheses (round brackets) are those of the original edition. Wyse-Power provided only three footnotes which are marked with asterisks and printed here as footnotes at the bottom of the relevant pages. Our own numbered notes are given as endnotes on pp. 176–9. We have silently corrected a few small typographical errors.

DONAL MCCARTNEY

PAURIC TRAVERS

WORDS

OF THE

DEAD CHIEF:

BEING

EXTRACTS FROM THE PUBLIC SPEECHES AND
OTHER PRONOUNCEMENTS OF

CHARLES STEWART PARNELL,

FROM THE BEGINNING TO THE CLOSE OF HIS
MEMORABLE LIFE.

COMPILED BY

JENNIE WYSE-POWER,

WITH AN

INTRODUCTION BY MISS ANNA PARNELL,

AND A FAC-SIMILE OF PORTION OF MR. PARNELL'S
FAMOUS MANIFESTO TO THE IRISH PEOPLE.

DUBLIN:
SEALY, BRYERS & WALKER
(A. THOM & CO., LTD.),
MIDDLE ABBEY STREET.

1892.

Dedicated
to
THE MEMORY OF THE DEAD

PREFACE

In preparing this little volume of extracts from the speeches and other public declarations of Mr Parnell, my aim has been to select such passages as were most characteristic of himself; of greatest significance in their bearing upon questions of practical politics, and of most vital importance for Irish Nationalists to study, to remember, and to take for guidance. Those who followed him when living will cling closer to his counsels, now that he is no longer left to lead them.

Before long, I hope, a more comprehensive volume of Mr Parnell's speeches will be prepared by some person better qualified for the task than I am, with better opportunities and with the advantage of happier times. Meanwhile, I dare to hope that this humble memento of the Great Leader will fulfil in some degree its purpose – to keep the principles which he enunciated before the minds of Irish Nationalists, for whom they should be a rule of political faith and conduct.

JENNIE WYSE-POWER

INTRODUCTION
Anna Parnell

'They are slaves who dare not be
In the right with two or three'[1]

Although the present political situation differs enormously from that prevailing at the time the first portion of these Extracts were spoken, there is still one significant feature in which they closely resemble each other.

In both cases we see a minority of the Irish Parliamentary Party in opposition to the majority, and found fault with by the latter on the ground that their action is displeasing to the English, and constitutes 'disunion' amongst the Irish themselves.

By doing nothing an Irish Party was least likely to irritate English sentiment; therefore, Mr Butt said nothing was the thing they ought to do, and in his day he believed as firmly in the efficacy of 'union' in doing it as Mr Dillon and Mr O'Brien now believe in the efficacy of 'union' in doing wrong.

For the tribute demanded in the joint name of the two Bogies, Irish Disunion and English Disapprobation, has been increased lately.

In Mr Butt's time nothing was asked for but the sacrifice of individual judgment – the sacrifice of reason in politics and the substitution of faith – on a question of expediency. This double-headed Moloch of ours *now* wants not only reason, but also principle, honour, justice, and self-respect offered up at its shrine.

On the question of expediency alone its present order is a pretty large one.

The right to govern our minds, if we have any, to make us eat, recant, and break, at a moment's notice, our most solemn and deliberate declarations, professions, and pledges; to choose which amongst us is to be allowed the privilege of crossing swords with them, all this must be conceded to the English.

And for what?

For an ostensible consideration that the persons who offer it are not now, and perhaps never will be, in a position to make good.

Suppose we allow Mr Gladstone to be perfectly sincere and trustworthy, what evidence have we that the English people, with whom the decision rests, will let him keep his promises? None whatever; any evidence there is on the subject is all the other way.

Nearly a hundred years ago Mr Pitt was going to give Catholic Emancipation, just as Mr Gladstone is going to give Home Rule to-day. Then, as now, a stiff payment in advance, the passing of the Union, was exacted for this concession, and it is said the consent of the Irish Catholic leaders to the Union was purchased by that bribe, Catholic Emancipation. We know how much they got it – as much as Home Rule will be got now by the sacrifice of Irish honour and that best part of independence, the foundation of every other kind, the independence of the mind.

So much for the ostensible consideration.

But supposing the ostensible consideration is not the real one?

If Irish MPs want places now, as they have been known to want them in the past, they are too numerous to be provided for now as they were in old times. There is only one way now to meet such a requirement, and that is by making Ireland itself supply the places.

Home Rule would do this, and if it supplied independence for the country also, all would be well. What we have to think of, however, is the danger of an arrangement that would contain no ingredient of Home Rule *except* those places.

The Scheme already introduced by Mr Gladstone made the repayment of the Imperial loan for buying out the landlords, and our contribution to Imperial expenses the first charge on our revenues, all those taxes which are easiest to collect and hardest to combine against, being taken for those purposes. If they also absorbed, as perhaps they might, all that the cultivators of land could afford to pay, there would be nothing left to carry on the Irish Government with except a balance representing the rack-rents that the cultivators can *not* afford to pay. At the same time the Irish legislature was so hampered and tied-up that it could not expect, as it might if it had a free hand, gradually to diminish the burden by increasing the wealth of the country through the development of her resources.

While that Scheme was before the English people the tone adopted by English Home Rulers in their speeches and their newspapers forbade the hope that it could become law in any but a deteriorated form, in which case there was every reason to fear that it would only prove an old device in a new dress, with the humorous touch added that the gratified aspirants to place would have to get their emoluments from a source most of them had spent a large part of their lives in trying to render unavailable.

The usual answer to views like this is, that the worst sort of Home Rule might 'lead to something else.' Certainly it might, but hardly to anything better, since the only weapon we have at present for extorting concessions, the interference of Irish members with English legislation, would be gone, and I cannot see what we should have instead. The most likely result would be that after some years of a hopeless struggle to make the system work, the Irish Government would break down in open disaster and confusion. England would then retake possession of us, in some way that would be free from the inconvenience to herself that her present form of tenure is now shown to involve; we should have our work to begin again from the beginning, and we should be more discredited than ever in the eyes of the world, as we should be held to have had self-government and proved unfit for it. Our liberation would then be postponed for a century instead of for a generation.

These are the trifling considerations on which we are told, in the name of Moloch, judgment should be allowed to go by default; the country should not even be asked to express an opinion about them. For Parliamentary elections, it must be remembered, are mainly expressions of opinions. There are eighty-six Irish National constituencies; because five of them have had an opportunity of speaking, their decision is to govern the other eighty-one!

I do not, it is true, wish to deny Moloch's right to any tribute whatever. I believe minorities should be as careful not to hamper majorities without sufficient cause, as majorities should be not to strain the patience of minorities by unreasonable exactions.

But I am no subscriber to the shibboleth now enjoying the honours of an axiom in our politics, that all Ireland's previous chances have been destroyed by 'disunion,' because I cannot see that 'disunion,' in its generally accepted sense, opposition offered by a minority of Nationalists to a majority, has ever once had such an effect, and there is at least one instance in our history where 'disunion,' had it been a little more stubborn, might have entirely changed our fate, There have been, certainly, efforts which might have had more success through a larger number of people joining in them, in earnest, but to this kind of union the other kind, consisting of slavish subservience to real or imaginary majorities, is a deadly enemy. What heart is likely to be in any Irish effort, when there is good reason to suspect that half its nominal supporters have no faith in it, but are afraid to say so?

However, there is a question before the Irish people more important than any question of expediency, a question of right and wrong, and here Moloch's territory ends, though its High Priests are making impudent claims to an extension of jurisdiction. The humblest minority owes no allegiance to the proudest majority on the smallest matter of principle. Rather, the more there are upholding the wrong, the fewer upholding the right, the more strenuously should the latter resist the triumph of the wrong, the more loudly should they make their voices heard on behalf of the right.

The question before the Irish people at present is: Can it be right first to lead a comrade into an ambush by false professions and promises, and insincere solicitations, then to desert him there, to hand him over to his enemy, and to help that enemy to destroy him? This is for Ireland to answer; she herself will be the sufferer if she gives a wrong answer.

ANNA PARNELL
January 23rd, 1892

Part I

The Early Struggles–The Land League

✦

'They never fail who die in a just cause . . .'
'Their spirit walks abroad'[1]

MEETING AT WHICH THE ELECTORS OF MEATH SELECTED MR PARNELL TO STAND FOR THEIR COUNTY

April 29th, 1875[2]

'With reference to the question of Home Rule, Mr Parnell said, that since he first could think he had the principles of that movement ever fixed in his heart, for he always believed that the day would come when the voice of the people in this country would rule her affairs, and make her laws, and that was what he understood by Home Rule.'

MAIDEN SPEECH ON COERCION BILL

April 26th [1875]

'In these discussions they always heard a great deal about exercising the rights of property, but they heard very little of the duties of those who held property. He had seen landlords sitting in polling booths watching the way in which illiterate voters recorded their votes, but he thought that could scarcely be considered either one of the rights *or duties* of landlords.'

DEBATE ON POLITICAL PRISONERS

House of Commons
July 8th [1875]

'Mr Parnell said he remembered the case of a man (Daniel Reddin), imprisoned for a political offence, who was suffering from paralysis, and who was believed to be shamming, and treated in a most inhuman manner. The unfortunate man was first subjected to an electric battery, and after that sharp instruments were run into the muscles of his legs. As soon as possible after the man was released from prison he commenced proceedings, but was met with the affidavits of medical men, who admitted that they were wrong, but contended that the treatment was justifiable, because they believed the man was shamming, and from that day to this there had been no chance of the unfortunate man having his case heard before the jury.'

House of Commons
July 27th [1875]

'There were many Irish members who believed that the House of Commons could never effectually legislate for Ireland.'

House of Commons
August 1st [1875]

'. . . In conclusion, he insisted that if England wanted to enforce a system of education on Ireland to which the people objected, they should pay for it themselves.'

August 10th [1875]

At a meeting of Amnesty Association, referring to the action of P. J. Smyth in giving directions to cut the traces of horses bearing Amnesty banner at the O'Connell celebration:

'Now he did not believe that Mr Smyth had any political sympathy with the men whom he had joined; that he really belonged to that Whig faction that sought to get possession of Dublin last week, and not only that, but to combine and turn the National sentiment of Ireland to the use of an insignificant, and he might add, dead party in Ireland.'

AT NAVAN

October 7th [1875]

'They did not want great speakers (in the House of Commons) but men who would always vote right.'

RESOLUTION PROPOSED BY C. S. PARNELL AT NOBBER

October 17th [1875]

'That we declare our continued and unalterable adhesion to the cause of Home Rule as defined by the great National Conference, to the cause of religious education, fixity of tenure, with fair rents, and amnesty to the political prisoners, and our abhorrence of any attempt, come from what quarter it may, to sow the seeds of dissension or division in the National ranks.'

During his speech on the same occasion, he said:

'The Irish people should also watch the conduct of their representatives in the House of Commons.'

POLITICAL PRISONERS' DEBATE

May 22nd, 1876

'With regard to Davitt, who was sentenced to fifteen years' penal servitude by a judge, I may say that the man who only got seven years was an Englishman; and I do not know how much effect Davitt's being an Irishman may have had with the judge (no, no). Hon. gentlemen may say no, but it is very hard to be superior to prejudice on all occasions, and I have little doubt that when this man was sentenced to fifteen years' penal servitude, the fact of his being an Irishman, and the fact of this occurring just after the Clerkenwell explosion,[3] and after the "murder" of Sergeant Brett,[4] which created a great deal of feeling in the minds of the middle and upper classes of this country, I have no doubt that fact had an effect.'

DEBATE ON THE MUTINY BILL

April 17th [1877]

{One of the first notable efforts of Mr Parnell to resist 'the sense of the House', was his opposition to flogging in the army. Although fiercely assailed by members of all sections, he persisted in his course, and finally 'killed the cat'.}

'It would be time enough to discuss the amount of flogging for garrotters and wife-beaters when that subject occupied their attention, but it was surely not desirable that gallant soldiers should be classed with those criminals. If there was one thing which had made a great impression on him in reference to this subject it was reading the account an officer gave of the first time he witnessed the punishment inflicted on as good and brave a soldier as ever stepped in uniform. The man had gone through the Crimean war, the Kaffir war, and the Indian mutiny, but because he was carried away by that desire for drink so common to cold climates, he was lashed to the triangle, and flogged in such a way, that strong healthy men fainted at the sight. He (Mr Parnell) denied that even a garrotter ought to be flogged, and he hoped the right hon. gentlemen would yield to the dictates of humanity, and reduce the punishment, which it was seldom necessary to inflict on gallant soldiers.

'He proposed that the limit of solitary confinement should be seven days, and an interval between such confinement of not less than fourteen days. To many temperaments solitary confinement was a more fearful punishment than the cat, and, indeed, temporary insanity had been known to ensue. He would provide that out of each 365 days of penal servitude in no case should a prisoner suffer more than 49 days' solitary confinement.'

PUBLIC MEETING AT BURSLEM, STAFFORDSHIRE

September 8th [1877]

{Already Mr Parnell had decided that the Irish Parliamentary Party should hold aloof from all English influences. He gave expression to his views very plainly.}

'It was a matter of history that Irishmen were not valued until they learnt to betray, but because the so-called obstructives had endeavoured, in so far as their limited capacity went, to do what they thought to be right, they were told that they were disgracing Ireland. At all events they had this satisfaction, they knew very well that Ireland did not think they were disgracing her . . . The Irish members (the followers of Mr Butt) said we must behave as the English members behave, in fact we must be Englishmen; we must go into English society and make ourselves agreeable and not cause a ruffle upon the smooth sea of parliamentary life, lest we forfeit our position as gentlemen and as members of the British House of Commons. Mr Biggar and himself, however, thought that that was a wrong view to take, and that it would be better for them always to remember that they were Irish representatives.'

AT KILMALLOCK

September 17th [1877]

'I often think that if we had the spirit that animates any one hundred men in this crowd – if we had that spirit in the English

House of Commons, that we should not have to come back year after year with nothing to bring back with us to Ireland . . . It is only Irishmen in the House of Commons who never can be Irishmen . . . It is not to conciliate, it is not to beg, it is not to crave that we are Irishmen, and Irish representatives. No, our duty is to demand, and if we will not get what we ask by demanding it, then our duty is to show them that they must give it . . . The Irish people are all of one mind on this question, or, if they are not to-day, I tell you, fellow-countrymen, they will be very soon of one mind on this question. I will bow to the decision of the Irish people, whether it be for or against me . . . We, none of us, can do any good unless the Irish people stand behind us, but if the people stand behind us I care not for the threats of the Chancellor of the Exchequer[5] – those funny old womanish threats; I care not for the threats of any Englishman. We shall show them that with the Irish people at our back we shall meet their threats with deeds.'

AT GREENOCK

September 22nd [1877]

{He expresses his belief in the possibility of success by vigorous action in Parliament.}

'They should carry out a vigorous and energetic policy, that Irishmen had always carried out in every place except the House of Commons. If that were done he believed they had a power in Parliament that few men had any notion of at present.'

AT NAVAN

September 24th [1877]

'The time will come when Ireland will see that great good may be done for her by a united band of Irishmen acting like men and Irishmen for her, on the floor of the House of Commons . . . He thought that opposition to English rule was best which was most felt. He thought that opposition was best which brought about results; and he thought that opposition was best which was determined and never flinching. The independent opposition of Gavan Duffy and Lucas failed because it was thwarted by treachery, for the English Government used means which it has always known how to use to thwart Irish opposition . . . Irish manhood could not die out; Irish national feelings could not die out. Although a party might disappear, although a party might do what was wrong, still they had the country behind them, and the people who lived in that country to fall back upon . . . O'Connell gained Catholic emancipation outside of the House of Commons, but he died brokenhearted, and left the work to other hands . . . but the premium for Irish dishonesty and corruption is not so high or so easy of attainment as it was in those days . . . No amount of eloquence could achieve what the fear of an impending insurrection – what the Clerkenwell explosion and the shot into the police van had achieved.'

AT BELFAST

September 27th [1877]

'It was simply impossible to put down Irish members, because they behaved themselves like men. The only way to put them down was the way in which Irishmen had always been put down. They had been bribed not to do their duty, but if they entered on a different course, and were independent – were real Irish members – it was impossible to put them down.'

HOME RULE CONFERENCE

January 15th, 1878.

'He did not think that they (the Irish members) should guide their action by any consideration of what the Government wished them to do; they should act in the interest of Ireland first, and if they could not act in the interest of Ireland without offending the House of Commons or without offending the Government, he told them they should act so all the same.'

THE MUTINY BILL

House of Commons
March 29th [1878]

'Last year some of them had considered it their duty to call attention to various punishments inflicted on soldiers. It was true then punishments had been passed year after year without remark, but this was no reason why it should be passed again. Still when he and some other members drew attention to the matter last year, the War Secretary[6] and the London Press had worked themselves up into a great state of indignation, which was reciprocated by a good number of members of the House. . . . He was sure there was no soldier in the House who would not rather have a swift and sure death at the hands of his comrade than face the slow gradual death that might await him in one of Her Majesty's convict establishments. The death of Sergeant M'Carthy[7] had affected him in a way he would never forget, and had forced on him the conclusion that soldiers should have the option of suffering death instead of enduring the lifelong torture of being confined with felons in a convict prison.'

DEBATE ON PUBLIC BUSINESS

May 28th [1878]

'They read in history that when Henry VIII wanted money he strode into the House of Commons, looking fiercely from side to side and saying, "I will have your money or else your heads." The Chancellor of the Exchequer adopted a somewhat similar course. The only difference was, that when he strode into the House, instead of saying, "My money or your heads," he said "I will have my money or I will have your day." That was the threat which the right hon. gentleman held out to the Irish members, and it was a threat which he thought the Irish members ought not to submit to.'

DEBATE ON VOLUNTEERS FOR IRELAND

June 13th [1878]

'He said there was no desire to attribute cowardice to the English soldier, but it was a common saying that in the day of battle the Irish regiments went first to break the line, the Scotch follow to take the prisoners, and the English came last to pick up the booty, which probably accounted for their having been able to acquire wealth more than the people of Ireland. It was unjust to refuse Ireland the right of defending herself while she was compelled to contribute to the defence of England.'

HOME RULE CONFEDERATION

October 21st [1878]

{The proper policy – to use the Irish vote for purely Irish ends.}

'There was no doubt that they could hold the balance of power between the two political parties in England, for which they only required a controlling power in 50 constituencies, He promised them he would use the power they had entrusted to him relentlessly against the opponents of Home Rule in Great Britain, irrespective of political party, and with the sole object of using the Irish vote for purely Irish ends.'

HOME RULE MEETING, ROTUNDA, DUBLIN

October 22nd [1878]

{From the first, Mr Parnell foresaw and dreaded the effect of English influences upon Irish members. How fully his fear was justified, recent history gives proof.}

'He wanted the country to know its own mind above all things, and when the country knew its own mind he wanted to see the country all united in carrying out that mind, whatever it was . . . But, if knowing what she had to do, she hesitated in carrying it out, the country would suffer for years to come . . . The energetic section (of Irish members) was made up of a small number of men, and the work was so hard that if he lived out this Parliament he expected to have lived a very long life indeed, in consequence of the work that had to be done. But the constituencies would have the power of sending them assistants, if they did not, it would not be the fault of himself and his friends . . . The air of Westminster would demoralize anyone, no matter how imperceptibly. As the air of London would eat away the stone walls of the House of Commons, so would the atmosphere of the House eat away the honour and honesty of the Irish members. Therefore they should send the best and truest men they could select to represent them, for they all felt the demoralizing influence of the atmosphere of Westminster.'

AT HOME RULE LEAGUE

February 3rd, 1879

'There can be no doubt that the more every Irish member keeps aloof from private communication with English ministers the better, but at the same time I am free to admit that circumstances may arise when you cannot help holding such communication. An English minister may come to you, and what are you to do? . . . The man who speaks in favour of a measure impedes that measure, equally with the man who speaks against it, and diminishes its chance of passing by so much time as he occupies in that speech . . . If the Liberals were in power to-morrow, the Irish party would have the balance of power, and if that party had common honesty, if it did not do as the Keogh and Sadlier party of 1852 did – of course then the position would be a very plain one to compel the redress of Irish grievances – but you may not have a balance of parties for the next twenty years . . . But so long as any Government, whether Conservative or Liberal, shows that it is mindful of the rights of our country by giving a reasonable portion of the time of the session to the settlement of some leading Irish question, then I see no reason why we should be unfriendly or hostile to them. But the moment that that favourable action ceases, then I think it is the duty of the Irish party to show their teeth, and not only to show their teeth, but to show that they can bite, and I think it is the duty of the Irish leader to find out some way in which that powerful Irish party can bite . . . I should like to see a little more disregard of what English members or English masters say, or even what English newspapers may say or think about our action. If we know that we are doing right, and if we can see that we are gaining results good for the country, why not do it guided by no other consideration than this. I admit that it is a very difficult position to rise superior to the public opinion of four or five hundred men, many of them of fine social position and very good education, some of the most distinguished in the world, but it is not difficult if the Irish member brings over with him to London some recollection of the exertions and sacrifices that have been, and that are being made by the people at home. If he can think of these things it will often keep him straight, when he may have a tendency to a little weak-kneedness, and perhaps go astray, more out of softness and good nature than any other motive. If he steels his heart against these influences which are brought to bear against every Irish member, and which constitutes one of the great weaknesses of the Irish Parliamentary representatives, you may depend on it, you will have your Irish member, instead of coming home empty-handed as in the past, as long as they are compelled to go over to London to legislate for you, they will return at least with some gifts from the Saxon ... I do not think concessions will demoralize the country if they are obtained in the right way, obtained without cringing or surrendering our national rights.'

IN THE HOUSE OF COMMONS

February 13th [1879]

'It was a matter of history that concessions were not to be won from any English Government by a policy of conciliation.'

House of Commons
February 19th [1879]

'What was it that made such a vast number of members obedient to the Government and ready to follow them? It was more or less the system of patronage which either directly or indirectly had permeated every branch of the Government, whether army, navy, or civil service, and in fact its influence extended to the Church. It further extended itself to the policy of the Government. Whether at home or abroad there was no department, however minute, upon which patronage had not its effect. It was not reasonable to suppose therefore that ministers would lightly give up a weapon which was of so much importance to them, and which they knew so well how to use.'

House of Commons
February 25th [1879]

'The House of Commons had a great history, and although Irish members might think their country had been injured by the necessity of having to seek justice in an English legislature, they could not look back upon that history without feelings of some reverence for it, and for the exertions of the men who had raised the House to the position which it now occupied. But what were the Government now proposing to do? They were going to drive a nail into the work of their ancestors – men who won their liberties and who fought for them. It remained for the despised Irish to insist upon preserving the rights and liberties of the House.'

House of Commons
February 27th [1879]

On the motion for a vote of £1,500,000 to defray the expenses of the war in Zululand, Mr Parnell said

– 'Sir, I wish to protest against the voting of this sum. I am aware my protest will not have any effect, but I feel I would not be discharging my duty to myself or to my constituents if I did not protest against this unjust and flagitious war. You have invaded a country inhabited by a people who have done you no harm, and you have deliberately prepared this invasion. It has been the policy of Her Majesty's Government to provoke this war, and to annex at all events a portion of the territory belonging to those Zulus.'

House of Commons
March 4th [1879]

'The noble lord, the member for King's Lynn (Lord Claud Hamilton) to-night spoke of a large section of the Irish people as being ignorant and bigoted. Now, Sir, if a large section of the Irish people are ignorant, it is due to the action of the party of which the noble lord is a member – an action which for centuries has deliberately kept that people in ignorance. But I deny, sir, that the people of Ireland are bigoted – I stand here as a sample of this – and I bear testimony to the fact that I, a Protestant, a member of the disestablished Church of Ireland, and a member of the Synod, represent the Catholics of Meath. Let the noble lord, when he charges the Irish people with bigotry, show from amongst his own countrymen such an example as this.'

House of Commons
March 6th [1879]

. . . 'As to the constabulary. If they had a minister responsible for that body, they would soon succeed in abolishing both the minister and the constabulary. Everybody must condemn the maintainance of an armed force, armed with weapons of precision – breech-loaders; he was not aware whether they had yet got Martini-Henry's – but with sword bayonets and all equipments necessary to take the field, except heavy artillery, which he had no doubt they could borrow if necessary. Such a farce was a contravention of the Mutiny Act, and against all constitutional precedent, and yet money was voted for it by this House year after year under the pretext that the people of Ireland were disorderly, that they required 15,000 armed and drilled soldiers to keep them in order.'

DEBATE ON PROFESSORS IN MIXED COLLEGES
AND UNIVERSITIES

March 14th [1879]

'Roman Catholics were entitled to their own opinions, and it was not to be expected that though the House might assimilate the system of education, Catholics could conscientiously send their children to mixed colleges . . . The system in Oxford and Cambridge was most sectarian, and he did not see how it was possible with a great variety of branches of knowledge, that teaching could be conducted from any other than a religious point of view. Were they going to have no history at all taught in their universities? Were they going to have no theological or divinity schools in order that they might carry out their peculiar ideas as to university education in Ireland? He said, by all means let the freethinker's children be taught in accordance with the freethinker's wish, but that the children of Roman Catholic parents be taught in accordance with their wish, and the children of Protestant parents in accordance with theirs.'

DEBATE ON INDICTABLE OFFENCES

April 3rd [1879]

'It always appeared to him to be a relic of barbarity that they should never have allowed an appeal in criminal cases. The case of the young man Habron[8] was an example of the enormous value that would be derived from a full and free appeal in criminal cases.'

AGRICULTURAL DEPRESSION IN IRELAND

May 27th [1879]

{This extract is specially worthy of note as being the first Parliamentary pronouncement made by Mr Parnell on the land question.}

'Owing to the great depression and to the competition of the American Market in corn, meal, and butter, the profits of the farmer had gone down considerably and he knew that both the graziers and small farmers experienced the greatest difficulty in making both ends meet. He believed that even on fairly rented properties it was a necessity for the tenant to have such security of tenure as would develop to the fullest the capabilities of the soil. Ireland at present was not more than one-third cultivated as it ought to be, and even its cultivated lands ought to produce three times as much as they did. It was necessary for the House how best to consider a measure of protection for the industry and exertion of the tenant – a measure of protection for the value which he added to the land; and he had no hesitation in saying that they must be prepared to adopt an exceptional measure of land reform for Ireland as compared with England.'

DEBATE ON SCOTCH PRISONS

June 9th [1879]

'If, as had been said, a prison was a reformatory establishment, it was exceedingly necessary that the warders should be of a better class than at present, and to secure that they must be sufficiently well paid. It had always appeared to him that the professional warder should be something like the professional schoolmaster. The great majority of prisoners were persons committed for the first time, therefore capable of reformation, and if warders of an inferior class were set over them, those prisoners would be hardened in crime instead of being reformed. If they trained warders as they trained schoolmasters they would have a better class of men, they would hear fewer complaints of them, and they would have more reformed prisoners.'

ALLEGED CRUELTIES IN ZULULAND

June 12th [1879]

'When you make war on a savage nation, it follows that your soldiers will also become more or less savage, and when they see their own countrymen massacred it is almost impossible to restrain them, and, therefore, her Majesty's Government should be careful not to enter into a war with a savage people unless compelled by the most urgent necessity to do so.'

ARMY REGULATION BILL

June 19th [1879]

'He appealed to the Secretary for War to mark his government by the noble deed of abolishing the flogging of the British soldier . . . Mr Parnell said that as three right hon. gentlemen – the Secretary for War, the First Lord of the Admiralty, and the Home Secretary[9] – were present it would be well for them to describe to the House, if possible, the nature of "the cat" used in their respective departments. They were told that there was a sealed pattern at the Home Office, and the Secretary for War had now promised to forward a sealed pattern to the War Office. He feared, however, that the right hon. gentleman knew little of the matter, but though that might be so it was very desirable for the House to be made aware of the character of that instrument of torture.'

DEBATE ON THE MILLTOWN MEETING

June 26th [1879]

'Under the circumstances that had been stated it was their duty to bring this subject before the highest tribunal in the country, because if the Government persisted in assisting the Irish landlords to collect rack rents from the people at the point of the bayonet, they would have murderous outrages in that district of the country. If the Government were supported in their course of oppressing the people consequences would follow that everyone must deplore. He knew that Government had great power, but the people also had great power when right was on their side, and the people in Mayo and other counties of Ireland would stand justified in using every means of passive resistance that they could to the minions of the law, and in order to enable them to live on the soil which God gave to them, where they were born, and where their children had a right to live'

THE ARMY BILL

June 19th [1879]

'He objected to making soldiers brave by the lash, and for his own part he believed that if a soldier preferred flogging to death, it would be that he might have the opportunity of shooting the officer who ordered it . . . He moved an amendment to the effect that flogging should be discontinued when the skin was broken or blood-drawn, and that no flogging stopped for any cause should be afterwards completed.'

AT ENNIS

June 20th [1879]

'They believed that by refraining from attaching themselves to any English party, and by opposing every English party that refused to do justice to Ireland, they could compel justice to be done to this country.'

LETTER FROM MR PARNELL, WHICH APPEARED IN
FREEMAN'S JOURNAL, 6TH AUGUST, IN REFERENCE
TO THE FAMOUS 'PAPIST–RAT' CONTROVERSY

[1879]

'Mr Gray has chosen to repeat over his name most painful imputations already contradicted by me as absolutely false, when first they appeared in his columns. It is needless to say that my contradiction remains unshaken. This reiterated attempt to steal away my character amongst my Catholic fellow countrymen is only one incident in the Whig intrigue for which the Irish National Party is already prepared, and which will be thoroughly understood by means of the series of public meetings now rendered necessary throughout the constituencies during the recess.'

HOME RULE DEMONSTRATION, HELD IN
THE CRYSTAL PALACE, LONDON

August 10th [1879]

'They desired the English people to inquire into the Irish questions, and they were convinced that when this was done they would see that justice, right, and truth were on the side of the Home Rulers . . . They should not be thought of too hardly if they spent a portion of their spare time in the House of Commons in improving the laws of England and bettering their civilization. If they had been enabled practically to abolish the lash in the British army it was because the Irish members had reason to know and remember the way in which their people had been flogged in 1798, during the Rebellion. If they were able to use the same effectual means for abolishing "the cat", it was because they were Irish members and not English; it was because they were dependent for their existence upon the public opinion of Ireland and not upon the public opinion of England. it was because they were able to survive the calumnies of the English Press, to live down, confident that truth was strongest in the end, and must prevail, that they kept on for three months telling the same story, until English newspapers who at first howled at them and ridiculed them came in the end to admit they were right.'

HOME RULE CONVENTION, LONDON

August 10th [1879]

'They had been charged with the attempt to break up the Irish Parliamentary Party, but he had always acted on the policy of sacrificing everything except what he considered vital national principles to the party of action in the House of Commons.'

HOME RULE MEETING, ROTUNDA, DUBLIN,

August 22nd [1879]

'I want to know if the people of Ireland desire this movement to end in the disreputable disgrace of 1852? (cries of no, no) . . . A notion that a great many of us have to get out of our heads is the notion that we are dependent on English public opinion and on English newspapers for our seats . . . When Ireland has an opportunity of sending seventy or eighty men to represent her, those men should be allowed to take that part in Parliamentary work which suits them best, and if one kind of work does not suit them well, then another kind of work will suit them. But, then, they ought not to interfere with the men who have work on hands, and believe in their work . . . Of course it is our duty – the duty of those men who believe and think with me – to do our very best until we are beaten. Of course if we find that we cannot bring the country with us, if we find that we cannot get a sufficient force of men to carry out our ideas, it will be our duty to give up Parliamentary agitation altogether, but when I give up Parliamentary agitation I don't promise to take to any other agitation. The future must be left to take care of itself.'

AT LIMERICK

August 31st [1879]

'The Land for the People'

'I firmly believe that, bad as are the prospects of this country, out of that we will obtain good for Ireland. . . It is the duty of the Irish tenant farmers to combine amongst themselves and ask for a reduction of rent, and if they get no reduction where a reduction is necessary, then I say that it is the duty of the tenant to pay no rent until he gets it. And if they combined in that way, if they stood together, and if being refused a reasonable and just reduction, they kept a firm grip of their homesteads, I can tell them that no power on earth could prevail against the hundreds of thousands of the tenant farmers of this country. Do not fear. You are not to be exterminated as you were in 1847, and take my word for it, it will not be attempted. You should ask for concessions that are just. Ask for them in a proper manner, and good landlords will give these conditions. But for the men who had always shown themselves regardless of right and justice in their dealings with these questions, I say it is necessary for you to maintain a firm and determined attitude. If you maintain that attitude victory must be yours. If when a farm was tenantless, owing to any cause, you refuse to take it, and the present most foolish competition amongst farmers came to an end, as undoubtedly it now must, these men who are forgetful of reason and of common sense must come to reconsider their position. I believe that the land of a country ought to be owned by the people of the country. And I think we should centre our exertions upon attaining that end . . .When we have the people of this country prosperous, self-reliant, and confident of the future, we will have an Irish nation which will be able to hold its own amongst the nations of the world. We will have a country which will be able to speak with the enemy in the gate – we will have a people who will understand their rights, and, knowing those rights, will be resolved to maintain them. We must all have this without injustice to any individual.'

AT LIMERICK

September 1st [1879]

'The Irish members are in a very peculiar position in Parliament. They are in London surrounded by influences which are not Irish influences, which are, on the contrary, hostile to every feeling, hope and aspiration that we all possess. We are cut off from your active sympathy and support while we are there struggling to do our duty . . . We are dependent above all things on the public opinion of this country, and we ought to be entirely independent of the public opinion of England, so long as that opinion clashes with the opinion of the people of this country.'

AT TIPPERARY

September 21st [1879]

'You must rely on your own determination, the determination which has enabled you to survive the famine years, and to be present here to day, and if you are determined I tell you you have the game in your own hands. Let there be no shrinking amongst you. I should be sorry to encourage you to be determined unless I thought that you could gain a great benefit by it yourselves and for the whole country; but I feel sure that the time has come when you can strike and help yourselves by standing together. I feel as convinced of this as of God's existence or my own . . . Bring public opinion to bear upon the landlords, exert every force of passive resistance to wrongful eviction, and you must win, for Providence is fighting for you.'

AT LIMERICK

October 5th [1879]

'While you are in the land is the time to take the necessary precautions in order to remain there, because a very good authority has told us, and an English authority, too, that 'possession is nine points of the law,' so that I think it is right that the people of this country should meet together and consider what course they are going to take where an unjust and unfair rent is demanded from them and insisted upon. Now I think you have the question very much in your own hands. If you stand together – if you remain firm – and if you refuse to pay an unjust rent, I say that the game is yours, and won already . . . Whether in the shape of unjust taxation or otherwise, so long as England has the power to govern you, so long will English ingenuity be directed to get the better of you in some way.'

AT NAVAN

October 12th [1879]

'You can never have civil liberty so long as strangers and Englishmen make your laws, and so long as the occupiers of the soil own not a single inch of it . . . I would merely say that the Parliamentary policy of an Irish patriot should be one sufficient and adequate to compel the attention of any English Government to the wants of this country . . . I will try to govern my conduct by the consideration of what you wish and desire me to do, and not of what any other body or collection of persons may desire me to do; and I feel confident that if you and Ireland send us assistance not many years will have passed by before we shall have exhibited our power in such a way as to show the English Government that they must no longer dare to trifle with the voice and wishes of Ireland.'

AT THE BANQUET IN NAVAN

October 12th [1879]

'The determination to act as if the eye of their constituencies were always upon them was the one thing necessary to enable the Irish Members to acquit themselves as they ought in the service of Ireland.'

AT NEWRY

October 16th [1879]

'If he could not trust his fellow-countrymen he would banish himself for ever from a country in which he could not feel that confidence which every right-minded citizen in a country must feel in order to do his duty by that country.'

AT WEXFORD

October 26th [1879]

'No man, however good, is fit to occupy the position of Irish landlord – no man, however good a Christian he may be – no matter how kind and humane-hearted he may be, is fit to be entrusted with the power that the law of the land entrusts to the Irish land-lord ... Let them send the dragoons as thick as the oaks in Shillelagh Wood, I tell you we shall beat the oligarchy in this country, who endeavoured to support a miserable and cruel system, and we shall beat them without the shedding of one drop of blood.'

November 2nd [1879]

'The tenant farmers have been very much to blame during the past years. They have paid patiently and uncomplainingly, unjust and exacting rents; they have taken farms from which tenants have been evicted, and paid unjust rents; they have been much in fault, but we must put a stop to that in the future. No man should take a farm from which another man has been evicted. No man should pay an unjust rent, whether he may have money in his pocket to pay it from his savings of past years or not, if the rent asked of him is not such as he has earned out of the farm in the past year; he must refuse to pay it, and he will be supported in that by the public and by the country . . . Stand fast by your homesteads, recollect you have the interests of your children to contend for, and if you are unequal to the task set before you, then you may be branded as men not deserving to live in these days. If, when Providence places at your hand an opportunity of securing for yourselves and for your children, and the future of all Irishmen, justice, happiness and prosperity. If you are too cowardly, too disunited to pluck the chance to take advantage of the opportunity, then I say there is no hope for Ireland.'

November 10th [1879]

'He looked upon the Irish Land question as being half-settled, because the people of the country had, as he had said, taken it into their own hands, and were showing happily that they understood the way in which that question must be settled . . . When Ireland had obtained her rights – when she had obtained her legislative independence – then it would be time enough for them to fulfil the functions of English citizens, and to cast in their lot with English political parties.'

AT ANTIENT CONCERT ROOMS, DUBLIN

November 19th [1879]

'There has undoubtedly been a great want of earnestness in the movement for the restoration of our Parliament. I regret very much to be obliged to admit it, but nevertheless it is not the less true that Irishmen have not shown that earnestness, that martyr-like spirit which it is necessary for every people to show who wish to gain the great and important rights that they ought to struggle for; and I think that one very great reason of that has been that in the municipal elections, and in the elections of Poor-law Guardians, in all the local government elections in Ireland, the question of self-government has been kept off the platform. In other countries where local self-government thrives, where it is carried out in its fullest perfection, where it almost approaches national self-government, we find that whenever there is a local government contest, the issue of that contest is looked forward to as a barometer indicating the political feeling of the country as regards the large national questions.'

MEETING AT ROTUNDA TO PROTEST AGAINST THE ARREST OF MESSRS DAVITT, DALY AND KILLEEN

November [21st, 1879]

'In O'Connell's time, when constitutional agitation seemed on the point of carrying Repeal of the Union, when all Ireland was to be gathered at the Clontarf meeting, the sword was flashed in O'Connell's face, and the meeting was stopped . . . But this movement will not be mastered; it does not depend on one man alone; it depends upon the will of our people; and they know too much now to abandon the path that has proved so formidable to the strongest Government that ever held power in England. The trick of trumping up charges against an Irishman is a very old one, and we are used to it by this time.'

AT BALLA

November 23rd [1879][10]

'The whole landed aristocracy of England and of Ireland also recognise that the movement that was begun last February on the plains of Mayo, at Irishtown has set the handwriting on the wall for the downfall of the most infamous system of land tenure that the world has ever seen. . . . The power of no man can prevail against a self-respecting and self- relying people.'

{In December, 1879, Mr Parnell left Ireland on his first public visit to the United States.[11] The purpose of his journey was to raise funds for the famine-stricken people at home, and to secure the sympathy and active support of the Irish race in America for his active policy.}

Replying to the presentation of an address from his admirers in Chicago January, 1880,[12] Mr Parnell said:

'Our task is of a double character. We have to war against the system which produces discontent and suffering in our country, and we have to endeavour to break down that system, and, with God's help, we are determined to break it down. We have also to see that the victims of this system are not suffered to perish in the meanwhile. We are to take care that the unity and strength of our people is not broken, and that now, when the opportunity has really come for the settlement of one of the leading questions in Ireland, that opportunity may not be lost.'

During an interview with a *New York Herald* reporter he said:

'Ireland never won any great reform except by agitation, and this agitation, like obstruction, has been necessary in order to gain the attention of the Government. When a Government or a country totally disregard you, you must use strong and even disagreeable measures to get their attention. The methods may be distasteful, but they are imperative . . . Experience has shown that England will not pay any attention to Irish affairs until the position has become unbearable to herself . . . A true revolutionary movement in Ireland should, in my opinion, partake of both a Constitutional and an illegal character. It should be an open and a secret organization, using the Constitution for its own purposes, but also taking advantage of its secret combination. But the leaders of the Fenian movement do not believe in Constitutional action because it has always been used in the past for the selfish purposes of its leaders.'

AT MADISON SQUARE GARDENS, NEW YORK

January 4th, 1880

'While we take care to do the best we can – and the best we can will be but little – to relieve the distress, we must also take care that we take advantage of the unexampled opportunity which is now presented to us for the purpose of sweeping away the bad system. In '47 America came forward first among the nations with unexampled liberality. But did that liberality prevent the famine? Did it prevent the millions from dying of starvation, or of the pestilence which follows famine? Did it prevent the scenes in Ireland in those years – the scenes on board the emigrant ships? No. No charity which can be given by America will avail to prevent Irish distress. That must be the duty of the British Government, and we must see that we shame that Government into a sense of its obligations. Are we to be compelled continually every 10 or 12 years to appear as mendicants before the world . . . Now it was proved in years gone by, and it has been proved frequently since that, that the Irish tenant will die in the ditch rather than enter the poorhouse. And he is right. The Irish Poor-law system is the most fiendish and ingenious system of all those that we have received from England, for the purpose of slowly torturing our country to death. The ties of a family are broken up. The father is separated from his children, the children from their mother, the wife from the husband, and the wretched inmates of the workhouse from the day they enter it are consigned to what is for many of them but a living death. "Ye who enter here leave all hope behind" might aptly be written upon the portals of every workhouse in Ireland . . . If, as we have been so frequently advised, we allowed the present opportunity to go by without any attempt at organization, we should have had a repetition of '47 and its terrible scenes. Government neglect would have been the same as ever, the hearts of the people would have been broken by physical suffering and distress, they would have been disorganized and exasperated, evictions in multitudes would have taken place, retaliatory action would have been adopted by the frenzied masses, we should have had another ineffectual rebellion, and 'the wild justice of revenge' would have been invoked against Irish landlords. But what a contrast have we. Instead of chaos and disorganization, the Irish people now present a remarkable aspect, firm, confident, and self-reliant; with death literally staring them in the face, they stand within the limit of the law and the constitution, and the first to set them the example of breaking that law has been the very Government of the country, which has sworn to do only that which is right. The attention of the whole civilized world is centred upon Ireland, and very shortly the merits of our question will be known in all parts. We have saved the lives of the landlords, and we have saved the lives of the people.'

AT THE GRAND OPERA HOUSE, NEWARK, NEW JERSEY

January 6th [1880]

'We are not permitted to have a single regiment of volunteers. The Government know very well that if there were Irish volunteers in Ireland, the land system would not be in existence – and the police and soldiers would not be allowed to shoot down women and children.'

In reply to an address from a deputation of the men of Meath, who waited on him in New York, Mr Parnell said:

'When other counties in Ireland have gone wrong, Meath has always been remarkable for the steadfastness with which she has stood by the true political faith. When the priests and electors of Athlone condoned the treachery of Judge Keogh, and by that condonation assisted the English Government to wake[13] up the independent Opposition movement of 1852, the priests and people of Meath assisted Lucas and Duffy in their great work.'

AT PHILADELPHIA

January 11th [1880]

'We must push the cause in Ireland, in England, and in America. We must push it everywhere, for all the world over are to be found our countrymen, and the heart of every one of them beats true to Ireland. We must encourage the people at home to stand firm and not be afraid. We must show them sympathy. We must let them see that we are determined to break down this odious land system which hangs like a horrible miasma over Ireland, and has prevented the development of energy and made the people listless and despondent.'

IN CONGRESS

February 2nd [1880]

'The public opinion of America will be of the utmost importance in enabling us to obtain a just and suitable settlement of the Irish Question . . . The most pressing question in Ireland is at the present moment the tenure of the land. The question is a very old one, it dates from the first settlement of Ireland from England. The struggle between those who owned the land on the one side and those who tilled it on the other has been a constant one, and up to the present moment scarcely any ray of light has ever been let in upon the hard fate of the tillers of the soil in that country . . . These Irish famines will have ceased when the cause has been removed. We shall be no longer compelled to tax your magnificent generosity, and we shall be able to promise that, with your help, this shall be the last Irish famine.'

AT A BANQUET GIVEN BY THE CORK FARMERS ' CLUB

March 21st [1880]

{Mr Parnell returned to Ireland on the 21st March, 1880, having been obliged to hasten back owing to the unexpected dissolution of Parliament. He had achieved a magnificent success in America. At Queenstown and in Cork he had received a splendid welcome.}

'I will say in short during the two months of our stay in America – and I must remind you it is only three months since we left the shores of Ireland – we visited sixty-two different cities, that is a little more than one city a night; we had to do two cities on one night – we had Sundays when we had to go to church – so that we had several times to do more than one city a night. Between two of these cities we on one occasion travelled 1,400 miles, and during the two months we remained in America we travelled together something like 10,000 or 11,000 miles by land. This joined to the 6,000 miles of ocean there and back amounts roughly to 16,000 miles in three months, which is not so bad for a man. The net result of these sixty-two cities, excepting San Francisco and one or two other places which we had not an opportunity of visiting, was 200,000 dollars actually in the hands of our Committee in America, as already remitted to the Irish National Land League. I am not speaking of what is to come . . . I should never have thought of entering into these matters were it not for this system of unheard of misrepresentation – misrepresentation which I could not have credited if I had not seen it, and which the English Press indulged in, and which I am sorry to say has found a faithful imitation in some miserable, servile Irish journals' (A Voice – 'The *Freeman*.') (Another Voice – 'The *Cork Examiner*.') Mr Parnell – ' I mention no names. The verdict of history will decide the point which has been called in question here to-night; but I was going to say that I should not have alluded to this matter were it not that the channels upon which an Irishman ought to be able to depend for information in his own country have been denied him . . . You have had sympathy and practical help in abundance simply because the world recognised that you were the under dog in the fight; but if you deliberately choose to remain the underdog, can you expect anything better than that the outside world should have you to lie in the bed which you have chosen for yourselves . . . When our good friends tell us that the time is reached when the Irish people will agree and be of the same mind – that there shall be no difference of parties in this happy country, and that there shall be no difference of opinion upon any question whatever, I think what a happy country that will be, but I despair of arriving at that country on this side of the grave . . .'

AT KILDARE

March 22nd [1880]

'Let those who are determined to go forward confident in the justice of their cause, determined to compel and to force where they cannot persuade – let them stand upon one side, and let the poor mean-spirited creatures who shrink, and cower and grovel, let them remain outside and not injure our noble cause with their miserable and grovelling touch.'

AT THURLES

March 23rd [1880]

'Our people after having passed through a night of terrible length and darkness are at length beginning to see the dawn of day – they are beginning to understand that the land of Ireland was not given to a few men for their benefit, but that it rightfully belongs to those who by their labour have sanctified it, cultivated it, and made it fruitful. If we have courage to stand by these Divine truths we shall win our battle . . . My life has been before you. We believe in our work, and we want the people of Ireland to believe in their work also. We want your members to be earnest and to believe in themselves and their cause. We want them to be energetic and devoted to the cause of Ireland, to strain every nerve, and not spare themselves by day or night when it may be necessary. With work, courage and determination we feel convinced that all the great questions now before the country will ultimately gain solution.'

AT CORK

April 4th [1880]

'They could compel justice to Ireland from any English Government provided they sent men of determination and integrity to represent them. If they sent in the minions of English political parties they could not expect anything but to live in the slavery which surrounded them at present. In 1852 an independent Irish Party was formed, and then, undoubtedly, Ireland had the same chance that she had now. The Tories were in office in the previous Parliament, and so long as the Tories were in office the independent Irish Party held together; but no sooner did the Whigs come back to office than the independent Irish Party was split into sections. The Whig members took sides with the Government. Judge Keogh and Sadleir, who had sworn that they never would take office from the Government betrayed the interests of the tenant farmers of Ireland. It was to prevent a repetition of such conduct that he came to Cork.'

AT NAVAN

April 8th [1880]

'Meath never threw away any chance, but Ireland must not throw away her chance as she has thrown it away once or twice before, and the only way Ireland can obtain justice from any English Government is by compulsion. . . . The only way in which you can succeed by Parliamentary methods of representation is to have an independent, determined, and active representation . . . If you return men who will hold themselves aloof from all English parties, and who will make up their minds to strike at both sides impartially until they obtain the rights of the country, you will have taken the first step to show that you deserve the liberties which you claim.'

AT THE LAND CONFERENCE, DUBLIN

April 19th [1880]

'Recollect, however you may disguise your meaning, any compromise with the system of landlordism simply means the prolongation of that system.'

AT A PUBLIC MEETING IN THE ROTUNDA

April 19th [1880]

'I aspire to no leadership. I wish to work as in the past as one of the rank and file. I have worked hard to do my duty for this country, and I shall continue to do so as long as I live.'[14]

AT CLAREMORRIS

May 2nd [1880]

'It was impossible for the 600,000 tenant farmers to be overwhelmed if they combined together. It was impossible for even the tenant farmers of a single county to be thrust out if they combined.'

AT NAVAN

May 4th [1880]

{At the General Election of 1880, Mr Parnell was returned for the Counties of Mayo and Meath, and for the City of Cork. He chose to sit in Parliament as member for the southern constituency.}

'I have planted the banner of Irish Nationality in the city of Cork, with the waves of English misgovernment surrounding us on every side, and I believe that it is my duty to hold that banner and to hold Cork.'

MEETING OF IRISH PARLIAMENTARY PARTY, DUBLIN

May 18th [1880]

'I am one of those who believe that you will never be able to carry out the principle of partnership in land. The landlords have been placed there under the feudal system of land tenure. This system has, perhaps, worked well on the whole in England, and England may be presented as the example of a country where the feudal system has been attended with less evil than in any other country. I think Ireland may equally well be represented as the example of a country where the feudal system has been attended with most mischief and suffering. It is admitted on all hands that the system is a false one. What hope then can we have in perpetuating such a system in Ireland. I believe the attempt to be perfectly hopeless, and I believe that is one of the reasons why this question of land tenure has made so little progress. It is because you have been proceeding on false lines, because you have been talking about the mutual interests of landlord and tenant in the land, where it is impossible that their interest should be a mutual one . . . There is another and a greater reason why I think that land reformers ought to strike at the root of the land evil: that is, the system of land-lordism. I speak now from the national point of view in the highest sense of the word. There can be no doubt that one of the reasons, and the greatest reason, next to the religious question, which now I hope no longer exists, the greatest reason why the upper, and many of the middle classes in Ireland – I speak more especially of the Protestant body, to which I belong myself – have remained aloof from the National operations of Ireland, and have refused to give them assistance, has been the institution of landlordism. You cannot expect the landlords of Ireland to strike for the rights of Ireland as long as you supply them with every inducement for the main-tenance of the English system of government here by upholding this land system.'

PUBLIC MEETING AT ST JAMES'S HALL, LONDON

June 6th [1880]

'The attitude, he thought, of the Irish Party towards the present Government ought to be one of reserve, until they saw what the present Government was going to do in fulfilment of its pledges to Ireland, and in fulfilment of its ordinary duty as a Government. A distinguished member of the Irish Party said they ought to maintain an attitude of "watchful expectation." Yes. "Shut your eyes and open your mouth, and see what you will get." That was the attitude which the Irish Members had been adopting ever since the Union, and with very poor results, as far as the interests of their country and their constituents had been concerned.'

DEBATE ON IRISH RELIEF OF DISTRESS ACT

House of Commons
June 17th [1880]

'They had been too long in the habit of appearing before the nations of the world as beggars for charity, and there were many people, in fact the majority of the people of Ireland, who now thought that the time had come when this practice should cease, and that they should have an opportunity of living in their own country, and of prospering, from the natural riches and resources of the country – an opportunity which the laws of England had denied them for so long a period. What was the Bill of the present Government? It was a Bill which simply sought to carry out the policy of the predecessors of the present Government, a policy which consigned a quarter of a million of people to death by starvation . . . While he (the Chief Secretary[15]) was considering the question the people would be gone. It was impossible to stop it if the Government deliberately refused to provide the people of Ireland with employment. They were deliberately encouraging outrage and revolution if the Government deliberately showed itself insensible to the sufferings of multitudes. It lost its title to a responsible Government, and they could not blame the ignorance of the people of the West of Ireland if they should attempt to do for themselves that which the Government refused to do for them.'

DEBATE ON THE COMMITTAL OF MR BRADLAUGH [16]

June 23rd [1880]

'He could not believe that the Irish constituencies would desire their members to vote for the imprisonment of anybody. They knew the last time that motion was made it was against the late William Smith O'Brien, who was taken to the place to which he supposed the hon. member for Northampton would be taken. . . . He would conclude, as he had begun, by saying that he did not believe the Irish constituencies would wish even an atheist imprisoned.'

SAME SUBJECT

July 1st [1880]

'His religion, however, taught him (Mr Parnell) to be just and fear not, and although a man might be placed under a temporary cloud, or a temporary disqualification, he thought and felt convinced that in the long run if he acted according to the just dictates of his conscience every right-thinking man at home and abroad would ultimately come to his support . . . An appeal had been made to Catholic Ireland. They had been told that that little island was the last country that had resisted the inroads of Continental infidelity, and that unless they desired that that odious thing should creep into Ireland, they must keep Mr Bradlaugh out of the house. Well, that surely seemed to indicate a fear on the part of the Irish Catholics that their religion might be injured by Mr Bradlaugh's introduction into the House, but were they entitled really to look at it from that point of view? Were they as Catholics entitled to say, 'Because we are Catholics we object to Mr Bradlaugh'? They must recollect that exactly the same argument was used against their own admission. They were Catholics deprived of their civil rights for centuries. Why were they deprived from coming into that House? It was because Protestants feared that the admission of Catholics would injure the Protestant religion, and it was because the majority of Protestants began to see that even if they had that fear, it was an unworthy fear – a fear that they ought not to allow to influence them in considering the civil rights of their fellow-men – that Catholics were at last admitted to the same civil and religious rights as Protestants. They must never forget that in dealing with this subject if they once admit the principle that they were entitled to object to a man because his doctrines were likely to injure their religion, they struck at the very root of civil and religious liberty, and that was why he felt it his duty to do that which was perfectly odious to him. It was a personally odious task for him to undertake to vote for the admission of the member for Northampton, Mr Bradlaugh, to that House, but if he had to walk through that lobby by himself he should feel himself a coward if he refused to do so.'

DEBATE ON MR DILLON'S KILDARE SPEECH

August 23rd [1880]

'He believed that the Land League had been instrumental in preventing outrages on cattle, and also in preventing much worse outrages – viz., the taking of the lives of landlords by assassination. He believed the Land League had done more to preserve the lives of landlords than all the Peace Preservation Acts that were ever passed . . . He asked whether those who wished to remove Irish grievances were to refrain from their exertions merely because the

Chief Secretary for Ireland had shown his good will by intro-
ducing a measure which the Government had failed to carry?'*

DEBATE ON THE PARLIAMENTARY RELATIONS
BETWEEN ENGLAND AND IRELAND

'When they had got rid of the landlords as a source of disunion in
Ireland, which made it necessary to support English
misgovernment in Ireland – when they had taken away from the
landlords the right of inflicting injustice – they believed they
would then be as national as when they stood side by side with
Grattan and Lord Charlemont in the Irish Volunteers of 1782.'

AT ENNIS
{Boycotting defined and defended}

September 19th [1880]

'I have seen that the more independence the Irish Party showed, the
more respect it gained for itself and for Ireland . . . Now what are you
to do to a tenant who bids for a farm from which another tenant has
been evicted?' (Several voices – 'Shoot him.') 'I think I heard
somebody say, "Shoot him." I wish to point out to you a very much
better way, a more Christian and charitable way, which will give the
lost man an opportunity of repenting. When a man takes a farm
from which another man has been evicted you must shun him on the
roadside when you meet him; you must shun him in the streets of
the town; you must shun him in the shop; you must shun him in the
fairgreen, and in the marketplace, and even in the place of worship
by leaving him alone, by putting him into a moral Coventry, by

---

* The Compensation for Disturbance Bill, which was rejected by the House of
Lords.

isolating him from the rest of his country as if he were the leper of old – you must show him your detestation of the crime he has committed. If you do this you may depend on it there will be no man so full of avarice, so lost to shame, as to dare the public opinion of all right-thinking men in the country and transgress your unwritten code of laws . . . I would strongly recommend public men not to waste their breath too much in discussing how the land question is to be settled, but rather to help and encourage the people in making it, as I just said, ripe for settlement. When it is ripe for settlement you will probably have your choice as to how it shall be settled, and I said a year ago that the land question would never be settled until the Irish landlords were just as anxious to have it settled as the Irish tenants . . . But I stand here to-day to express my opinion that no settlement can be satisfactory or permanent which does not ensure the uprooting of that system of landlordism which has brought the country three times in a century to famine . . . We have been accused of preaching Communistic doctrines when we told the people not to pay an unjust rent, and the following out of that advice in a few of the Irish counties had shown the English Government the necessity for a radical alteration in the land laws. But how would they like it if we told the people some day or other not to pay any rent until this question is settled . . . If the 500,000 tenant farmers of Ireland struck against the 10,000 landlords, I should like to see where they would get police and soldiers enough to make them pay.'

INTERVIEW WITH MR JAMES REDPATH

September [1880]

Referring to debate on Police Vote, he said –

'The Government maintain in Ireland 21,000 soldiers and 11,000 policemen – policemen armed with rifles and bayonets, bullets and buckshot – and we wish to put an end to the pretence that this so-called civil force is anything else but an army of occupation scattered through the country in their armour-plated barracks and iron huts, to hold it for the landlords and the British. We insist that the mask must be torn off, and that if our people are to be evicted and shot down, it shall not be done by a disguised force of so-called policemen, but that England must do the work with her red coats, and with all the insignia of organized oppression . . . Before the elections the Liberals and Home Rulers had been sitting all together on the Opposition side of the House. After the elections, the victorious Liberals crossed the floor to the Ministerial side, and such of the Irish members as had leanings to or expectations from the Government followed them. I and my friends retained our old places in Opposition . . . With the kindliest Ministry in power, between the kindliest Minister and ourselves there is an impassable chasm. We wish to deal thoroughly with the land question and the Liberals. Why [While] their party is largely made up of Whig landowners, and as at present constituted can any measure initiated by a Government which these men maintain in power, thwarted as it must be by a compact Conservative Opposition, entirely composed of landlords, and with the gauntlet to be run through the House of Lords, which is merely a territorial trades' union, be at all likely to be adequate or satisfactory?'

AT A BANQUET IN CORK

October 3rd [1880]

'The toast of Prosperity to Ireland had been a somewhat familiar one to many newspaper readers in connection with the names of those who had the power of ruling over them. If there was one thing he was determined to do his humble endeavours to bring about, it was the power of the Irish people to govern themselves, so that in future they would not have to associate "the prosperity of

Ireland" with the name of a ruler sent from England . . . Ireland did not prosper and never could prosper until their right over land and sea, over everything in Ireland was given to them . . . He thought the attitude and demeanour of the Irish people in the present crisis was worthy of every commendation. There had been very little crime or outrage compared with the suffering they had endured. In fact, their people had always been patient. He did not like to say they had been too patient, though he thought their people had always been too patient, but the limit of their patience would some day be reached in reference to the Irish land system . . . To-day they were a party of independent opposition in the House of Commons, pledged to remain aloof from English parties, pledged in the words of Lucas to be a separate element in the Legislature, and if necessary disordering, disorganizing, and interfering, as it was expedient or possible, with every business that may be transacted. They could push this policy as far as they liked. They need not trench on it at all. They might keep the weapon in the scabbard, but the weapon was there; they had it at their command, and when all other resources failed it was as potent and powerful for a party of 40 against the present Whig Ministry as it was for a party of 70 against the last Tory Government.'

AT LONGFORD

October 17th [1880]

'I am not one of those who wish to attribute too great virtues to a Parliamentary policy, but I do think that so long as Irish members go to Westminster they had better go as Irish members, than as servants of the English Government . . . We are calling upon the Irish constituencies to send us a party to the House of Commons that will carry out the policy of Frederick Lucas to the bitter end if it should be necessary, and we promise you that such a party instead of being a byword and a disgrace to Ireland as it has been in times past, will at least be of some assistance to the noble exertions that the people are making to-day, and that when we have succeeded in destroying landlordism, the chief prop of English misrule, we may be able to go further until we have obtained the restitution of our legislative independence, robbed from us in 1800.'

AT A BANQUET IN GALWAY

October 24th [1880]

Replying to the toast of 'The Irish abroad,' – 'I feel convinced that if you ever call on them (the Irish in America) in another field, and if you can show them that there is a fair and good chance of success, that you will have their assistance, their trained and organized assistance, for the purpose of breaking the yoke which encircles you, just in the same way as you have had that assistance last winter to save you from famine.'

AT TIPPERARY

October 31st [1880]

'When you have a good harvest, then is the time to hold it. You had not had anything to hold last year, and perhaps the necessity for exertion was not so great as to-day, The people of Ireland have at last come to that. When they have sown the seed and reaped the harvest it is their duty also to look after themselves, their wives, and their children . . . We have been told that we are unpatriotic because we desired to make the tenants owners, but the same men who tell us we are unpatriotic because we desire to make the tenants owners after paying a Government rental for a limited number of years, do not see their own inconsistency when they propose that the same Government shall have the arbitration of what rent the tenant shall pay.'

AT LIMERICK

November 1st [1880]

{The frequency with which Mr Parnell referred to the probability of his party being tampered [with], is evidence that this danger was constantly before his eyes. He had not studied Irish history in vain, and, alas! his fears were but too well founded.}

'If you are afraid of a rent process you had better go out of the country altogether.'

Replying after the presentation of the Freedom of Limerick city being conferred on him:

'I am not one of those who believe in the permanence of an Irish party in the English Parliament. I feel convinced that sooner or later the influence which every English Government has at its command – the powerful and demoralising influence – sooner or later will sap the best party you can return to the House of Commons. I don't think we ought to rely too much on the permanent independence of an Irish party sitting at a distance from their constituencies, or legislating, or attempting to legislate, for Ireland in Westminster. But I think it is possible to maintain the independence of our party by great exertions and by great sacrifices on the part of the constituencies of Ireland, while we are making a short, sharp, and, I trust, decisive struggle for the restoration of our legislative independence.'

LAND LEAGUE MEETING, DUBLIN

November 4th [1880]

Referring to the action of Mr Forster in instituting the State prosecutions:

'I regret that he has chosen rather to waste his time, the money of the Government and of the people of Ireland, spent in defending the traversers in those prosecutions under the absolute law of conspiracy. He has begun in a bad way, and I fear that the result of his attempt to govern Ireland on these lines will be to shatter the reputation for statesmanship which he formerly acquired in another branch. He is surrounded by a landlord atmosphere at the Castle of Dublin, and although he may be able to resist the effect of that atmosphere longer than most men, yet, sooner or later, it is bound to tell on him.'

AT WATERFORD

December 5th [1880]

Referring to the settlement of the land question:

'Don't let us ask for anything that is impracticable or impossible. Don't let us ask for anything which has not been sanctioned by the successful example of almost every European country, and take our stand upon just rights – the ownership of the land for the people of Ireland. Let us leave to the enemy the offer of compromise; let the first offer of compromise come from them, for they are the beleaguered and isolated garrison . . . Every farmer who now lies down at the feet of the landlord is a traitor to his country.'

AT A BANQUET IN WATERFORD

On the same date

'We have the forces of nature, we have the forces of nationality, and we have the forces of patriotism and true devotion that have never been wanting in this land of ours, and I am sure these forces will be sufficient for the task which we all have before us, the task of breaking the neck of English misgovernment in Ireland, and chasing from the country the usurpation which has long had its heel upon our necks . . . A concession may be very good in its way where it prepares for something better, but where it perpetuates a bad and vicious system I think it is better to resist these concessions, and to prevent them from obtaining an entrance amongst us while there is yet time.'

1881

In an interview with a Press Association reporter, after being expelled from the House of Commons, he said:

'The Irish Secretary seeks to avenge himself upon us because he has been such a failure. He has found it impossible to persuade the Irish people that he and the English Parliament would govern them justly, and he is now trying to intimidate them into that belief. The Irish National Land League and the Independent Irish Party in Parliament are the chief obstacles in his path, and therefore he tries to rid himself of both one and the other.'

AT CLARA

February 20th [1881]

'I ask you not to be afraid of coercion; that weapon has already been broken, even before it has been raised to strike. I believe that the result of this last attempt at coercion will be the destruction of British misrule in Ireland . . . If you meet this policy by a policy of passive resistance; if you patiently suffer and endure anything that they put upon you; if you avoid retaliation, or the attempt to meet force by force; if you stand by and encourage each other in your sufferings; if you refuse to take farms from which your neighbours have been evicted; if you refuse to pay unjust rents, this measure of coercion will fall harmlessly upon you, and will recoil on the heads of its authors with crushing effect.'

DEBATE ON 'THE ARMS BILL'

March 4th [1881]

'I tell the Prime Minister back that crime dogs the footsteps of the evictors, and if you want to put a stop to crime you must put a stop to eviction. You will not succeed by this Bill in protecting landlords who violate every feeling of justice and mercy. You will not prevent outraged tenants from shooting their landlords. The Bill will increase the number of murders and outrages in Ireland, and it will also increase, as unhappily we have already seen, too evidently the number of evictions. It is of importance to you to conciliate the feelings of the Irish people; it is of importance that your Government should not be known to history and remembered in Ireland as the Coercion Government; it is of importance that the Irish people should not bear your rule in mind as a rule of petty tyranny and police; as a rule of magisterial oppression, as a rule of suspicion and not of law . . . The more you tyrannise, the more you trifle with the Irish people, the stronger will burn the spirit of nationality – the more they will free themselves from the yoke which renders such things possible. We may have our day – our short day of persecution. I believe the public opinion of the people of England will, at some day or other, do justice to our motives, even if they do not approve of our course.'

DEBATE ON SAME

March 13th [1881]

'They in Ireland would have to face the coercive measure of the Government the best way they could. He believed Ireland would emerge victorious from the strife. It was impossible in the present times of the electric telegraph and steam communication to coerce the public opinion of the country . . . After having asserted the dignity of the law the grievances are forgotten, and there is no consideration for them. This has been the case for over 200 years in

Ireland, and nothing has been done except under the influence of terror . . . The result of the present experiment would be to show the Government that they never made a greater mistake than when they attempted to use the worn-out weapon of coercion for the purpose of destroying the proper and constitutional expression of public opinion in Ireland.'

DEBATE ON THE LAND BILL

July 14th [1881]

'Mr Parnell said he did not know by what title the Chancellor of the Duchy of Lancaster (Mr Bright) presumed to tell, or dared to tell, the Irish Members, that they dare not vote against this clause. He (Mr Parnell) intended to vote against it, and he denied that the Chancellor of the Duchy of Lancaster had any right to impute to him, or to a majority of the members who were acting with him, any intention, by the course they were pursuing, or had pursued up to the present, of obstructing this clause, or any clause of the Bill.'

DEBATE ON THE ARRESTS IN IRELAND
{During which Mr Parnell was suspended}

August 1st [1881]

Mr Parnell said – 'The Ministry of the day, of course, always gain the sympathies of the powers that be in this House, and if we may not bring the cause of our imprisoned countrymen before this House, I may say that all liberty and regard of private right is lost to this assembly, and that the Minister of the day has transformed himself from a constitutional Minister into a tyrant.'

{The Speaker here named Mr Parnell as disregarding the authority of the House.}

Mr Parnell, speaking in a loud voice from the gangway said – 'I shall not await the farce of a division. I shall leave you and your House, and I shall call the public to witness that you have refused us freedom of discussion.'

DEBATE ON THE IRISH EXECUTIVE

August 18th [1881]

He said – 'It was a well-known fact, that were it not for the existence of the Land League, and the determination of the Irish people, not all the strength of that House, and all the force of public opinion in England, could have forced the Land Bill through the House of Lords. He thought, therefore, the Irish people would be wise if they continued to the end to rely upon those exertions which had produced for them such an instalment of their rights.'

DEBATE ON THE IRISH CONSTABULARY VOTE

August 21st [1881]

'Mr Parnell asked why the police in Ireland should go to evictions with fixed bayonets. What use could a bayonet be to a man in getting through a window? The constabulary, too, could be seen returning from evictions in a state of intoxication . . . Continuing, he asked if the Chief Secretary thought that he could get even Irishmen to beat unoffending women and children with the butt end of their rifles unless they were intoxicated? The police in Ireland had been carefully prepared for this duty. They were brought from different localities, and if any one of them exceeded his duty it was impossible for the people to identify him. Would the right hon. gentleman have any objection to the Irish Constabulary being numbered as the police were in England? The same protection that was afforded to English roughs should be extended to the peasants – women and children – of Ireland, viz., the opportunity of identifying Constables by the numbers on their collars.'

{During Tyrone election contest}

August 30th [1881]

{The significance of these few sentences is enhanced by the recent statement of one of the leading seceders, to the effect that when Mr Gladstone and the Liberal Party came back to power, the associates of Mr McCarthy would advise the Government on the bestowal of patronage in Ireland.}

'. . . I have said that Irish landlordism was one of the principal props of English misrule in Ireland. We have nearly cut and hacked that prop in two . . . But this system of Government patronage is also a very great prop, because by its means the Government of the day – I don't care whether it is Whig or Tory – but every English Government, of whatever political shade, has always by the means of patronage been able to destroy the independence of every Irish party until now. They have not succeeded in destroying the independence of the present Irish party; and I trust that we shall be able to prevent them doing so.'

MEETING AT GORTIN, CO. TYRONE

August 31st [1881]

'The Land Bill that we wish to see brought in is a Land Bill that will give the landlord whatever he has put into the land, and will give the tenant whatever he has put into it, and we feel confident that if such a Land Bill as that were brought in and carried, instead of the landlords getting £17,000,000 sterling a year of rent from

Ireland, they would not be entitled to more than £1,000,000 or £2,000,000 at the very outside. A Government Land Bill that aims at leaving the landlords all the plunder that they have succeeded in exacting from the farmers up to the present moment, that does not compel them to disgorge at least one-half of their ill-gotten goods, such a bill is a fraud, a cheat, and a mockery – such a bill is merely a shifting of the load from one shoulder to the other. We seek for Ireland the right to govern herself and we can only do this by stopping the corruption and place-hunting that is going on in the North of Ireland.'

MEETING AT DUNGANNON

September 1st [1881]

'If we could have an independent party in Ireland, we feel confident that instead of the slow and halting progress which we have witnessed in the path of reform since the Union, the cause of Ireland will advance by the leaps and bounds by which it has advanced during the eighteen months of the existence of the Land League. We ask no timid volunteer by the way to come along with us. We want men of true, firm, and strong belief in our cause, because we know from the teachings of history that every great cause has often been fatally damaged and sometimes permanently retarded by the timidity and want of belief of its disciples.'

MEETING AT FINTONA

September 2nd [1881]

'. . . Every member returned by an Irish constituency should hold himself aloof from every English political party, and refuse to accept any situation until it is in the power of the Irish people – I trust and believe it will be at no distant date – to give to their faithful servants suitable rewards . . . Remember there is no finality in politics, and that the politician who tells you to stand is effete. The progress of the people is ever marching on.'

SPEECH AT THE IRISH NATIONAL CONVENTION,
ROTUNDA, DUBLIN

September 15th [1881]

'If we had our own Parliament, with full powers, we should undoubtedly be invited to protect Irish manufactures by prohibitive or import duties – just as the United States of America, and every European Country also where industries were crushed in the bud at the end of the last century, and the beginning of this, by English legislation and English exactions, have protected their industry – against the settled industries of Great Britain. We should be invited, if we had the power of self-government, to do the same thing, and any movement that we set on foot to be successful must proceed on this principle. We cannot by the law of the land declare that Irish manufactures shall be protected, but we can protect them by our unwritten law, by the public and organised opinion of the great majority of the people of this country, in accordance with whose opinions all laws governing Ireland ought to be made, and if we resolve, if we bind ourselves together into an organization to protect Irish industries, depend upon it that Irish industries will flourish and thrive in Ireland, but in no other way can you succeed.'

SPEECH ON THE SECOND DAY OF THE CONVENTION

'Nothing could be more disastrous to our movement and to our organization, and to your hopes of getting your rents reduced, than any indiscriminate rush of Irish tenantry into court, and it is with a view to prevent this that we desire to take the tenantry in hands, and to guide them in this matter, because, depend upon it, if we don't guide them there will be others who will. If we don't take hold of the Irish tenantry and guide them for their advantage, there will be others who will guide them for their destruction.'

SPEECH AT MEETING OF THE LAND LEAGUE

October 7th [1881]

'I think that in every movement of this kind it is most desirable that there should be a large section considerably in advance of the rest. For my part, having been during several years of my political life considerably in advance of the rest of the country, I am exceedingly pleased to know, as the result of my explorations during the last few weeks, that the rest of the country is considerably in advance of me, and I don't in the least object to find men a long way beyond me, in fact I like it exceedingly.'

AT WEXFORD

October 9th [1881]

{The answer to this speech from Mr Gladstone was a warrant for Mr Parnell's arrest, under Mr Forster's Protection of Life and Property Act.}

'You have gained something by your exertions during the last twelve months, but I am here to-day to tell you that you have gained but a fraction of that to which you are entitled. And the Irishman who thinks that he can now throw away his arms, just as Grattan disbanded the Volunteers in 1782, will find to his sorrow and destruction when too late that he has placed himself in the power of a perfidious and cruel and unrelenting English enemy.'

Referring to Mr Gladstone's recent Guildhall speech he said:

'Not content with maligning you, he maligns your bishops, he maligns John Dillon. He endeavours to misrepresent the Young Ireland party of 1848. No misrepresentation is too patent, too mean, or too low for him to stoop to. And it is a good sign that this masquerading knight-errant, this pretended champion of the rights of every other nation except those of the Irish nation, should be obliged to throw off the mask to-day, and to stand revealed as the man who by his own utterances is prepared to carry fire and sword into your homesteads unless you humbly abase yourselves before him, and before the landlords of the country. But I had forgotten. I said that he maligned everybody. Oh, no. He has a good word for one or two people. He says the late Isaac Butt was a most estimable man, and a true patriot. When we in Ireland were following Isaac Butt into the lobbies, endeavouring to obtain the very Act which William Ewart Gladstone – having stolen the idea from Isaac Butt – passed last Session, William Ewart Gladstone and his ex-Government officials were following Sir Stafford Northcote and Benjamin Disraeli into the other lobby. No man is good in Ireland until he is dead and unable to do anything more for his country. In the opinion of an English statesman no man is good in Ireland until he is dead and buried, and unable to strike a blow for Ireland. Perhaps the day may come when I may get a good word from English statesmen, as being a moderate man, after I am dead and buried . . . When people talk of public plunder they should first ask themselves, and recall to mind who were the first plunderers in Ireland. The land of Ireland has been confiscated three times over by the men whose descendants Mr Gladstone is supporting in the enjoyment of the fruits of their plunder by his bayonets and his buckshot. And when we are spoken to about plunder, we are entitled to ask who were the first and the biggest plunderers . . . This doctrine of public plunder is only a question of degree . . . In one last despairing wail he says– "And the

Government are expected to preserve peace with no moral force behind it." The Government has no moral force behind it in Ireland, the whole Irish people are against them. They have to depend for their support upon a self-interested and a very small minority of the people of this country, and therefore they have no moral force behind them; and Mr Gladstone in those few short words admits that English government has failed in Ireland. He admits the contention that Grattan and the Volunteers of 1782 fought for; he admits the contention that the men of '98 died for; he admits the contention that O'Connell argued for; he admits the contention that the men of '48 staked their all for; he admits the contention that the men of '65, after a long period of depression, and apparent death of National life in Ireland, cheerfully faced the dungeon and the horrors of penal servitude for, and he admits the contention that to-day you in your overpowering multitudes have established, and please God will bring to a successful issue, namely – that England's mission in Ireland has been a failure, and that Irishmen have established their right to govern Ireland by laws made by themselves on Irish soil. And he wound up with a threat – this man who has no moral force behind him – he wound up with a threat – "No fear of force, and no fear of ruin through force shall prevail, as far as we are concerned, and it is in our power." I say it is not in his power to trample on the aspirations and the rights of the Irish nation with no moral force behind him. These are very brave words that he uses, but it strikes me that they have a ring about them like the whistle of a schoolboy on his way through a churchyard at night to keep up his courage. He would have you to believe that he is not afraid of you, because he has disarmed you, because he has attempted to disorganize you, because he knows that the Irish nation is to-day disarmed as far as physical weapons go, but he does not hold this kind of language with the Boers. At the beginning of the session he said something of this kind with regard to the Boers. He said that he was going to put them down, and as soon as he had discovered that they were able to shoot straighter than his own soldiers he allowed these few men to put him and his government down . . . I trust that as the result of this great movement we shall see that, just as Gladstone by the Act of 1881 has eaten all his old words, has departed from all his formerly declared principles, now we shall see that these brave words of this English Prime Minister will be scattered as chaff before the united and advancing determination of the Irish people to regain for themselves their lost land, and their legislative independence.'

AT A BANQUET IN WEXFORD

October 10th [1881]

Mr Parnell said – 'I am frequently disposed to think that Ireland has not yet got through the troubled waters of affliction to be crossed before we reach the promised land of prosperity to Ireland. If we had no one but our own selves to deal with, we should soon arrive at prosperity; but we have, unfortunately, another, a stronger and a more powerful nation outside our own nation, who assume to control our destinies, and we do not know what interference, what meddlesome interference we will have to meet from time to time in the future to retard our prosperity and prevent the attainment of that which we all hope and wish for . . . But I have every confidence that even the most bigoted Saxon will come to recognise that he is asking the great English nation to perform an impossibility when he asks that nation to attempt to rule our nation from English soil.'

In Kilmainham jail, immediately after his arrest, he said to a *Freeman's Journal* reporter – 'I shall take it as evidence that the people of the country did not do their duty if I am speedily released.'

[Symbol of harp in original edition]

Part II

From Prison to Victory

✦

'He has brought thee through deep waters,
Through the furnace, through the cloud'[17]

1882

Two days after Mr Parnell's release (4th May) from Kilmainham,
he made the following statement in the House of Commons in
answer to a speech of Mr Gladstone's: – 'In the first portion of his
(Mr Gladstone's) speech the idea conveyed was that if the hon.
members for Tipperary and Roscommon (Messrs. Dillon and
O'Kelly) along with myself were released we would take some
special action with regard to the restoration of law and order. I
assume that the right hon. gentleman has received information
from some of my friends to whom I have made either a written or
verbal communications with regard to my intentions upon the
state of this Irish question. But I wish to say emphatically that I
have not in conversation with my friends or in any written communication to my friends entered into the question of the release
of my hon. friends or myself as any condition of our action. (Cheers,
with which Mr Gladstone assented.) I have not, either in writing or
verbally, referred to our release in any degree whatsoever; and I

wish to call attention to the first statement of the Prime Minister in order to show that it conveyed – although I am sure the right hon. gentleman did not intend it should do so – the reverse of that fact. (No, no, from Mr Gladstone.) Still, sir, I have stated verbally to more than one of my hon. friends and I have written, that I believe a settlement of this arrears question, which now compels the Government to turn out into the road tenants who are unable to pay their rents, who have no hope of being able to pay rent for which they were rendered liable in the bad seasons of 1878, 1879, and 1880, would have an enormous effect in the restoration of law and order in Ireland – (cheers) – would take away the last excuse for the outrages which have been unhappily committed in such large numbers during the last six months, and I believe we, in common with all persons who desire to see the prosperity of Ireland, would be able to take such steps as would have material effect in diminishing those unhappy and lamentable outrages. (Ministerial and Irish cheers.) I desired, sir, to make this statement with regard to a matter of fact. I do not wish to enter into the debatable matter introduced by the right hon. gentleman the Chief Secretary for Ireland.'

In the course of an interview with a correspondent of the *Irish World*, immediately after his release from Kilmainham, Mr Parnell made the following statements in answer to the questions put to him: – 'There is no understanding then about the withdrawal of the No Rent Manifesto? None whatever. What will you do about it? We will do nothing until we find out what the Government propose to do – more especially as to the question of arrears. What do you think of the success of the manifesto? I think it has accomplished its purpose. Do you think open meetings of the League will be now permitted? That, of course, I cannot tell. But I think we formerly paid too much attention to meetings and too little to practical organization. One result of which was to push humbugs to the front and keep practical men behind. What is your view of the situation? The Government appear to have changed their policy entirely. Their action evidently indicates that coercion is to be condoned [condemned] or very much modified, and that fresh concessions of a valuable character are to be offered to the people. I feel convinced that if this opportunity, which has been presented to us be properly used, it will result in the working out of a practical solution of the Land question, and, after a little time, in bringing about an entirely new departure as regards English government in Ireland, in the direction of allowing the Irish to govern themselves. I am inclined to suppose that during some months past two opposite causes have agitated the Cabinet: first, the adoption of more extreme measures of coercion than this country has ever suffered from, in the shape of the abolition of jury trial, pecuniary penalties levied upon districts for outrages, and for the support of military occupation; and, secondly, the alternative proposition of the abandonment of coercion, and the offering of fresh concessions. The last policy having gained the upper hand, it has caused the retirement of Mr Forster. It is impossible for me, under these circumstances, to refrain from expressing my satisfaction with the situation, so far as it has been developed, but it is impossible to state what the future course of the Land League may be until we have ascertained more definitely the Government proposal. The ladies (of the Land League), I understand, now propose to retire. I don't know that they really will, but they must be greatly tired. They have had work and worry enough to make their heads white. It is impossible to say too much for the noble manner in which they have performed their work.'

To a representative of the Press Association, on the subject of the Phoenix Park murders, May 7th, he said:

'It seems to me as if there were some unhappy destiny presiding over Ireland, which always, at the moment when there seemed a probability of some chance for our country, comes in suddenly to destroy the hope of her best friends. I trust that the people of Ireland will take immediate and practical steps to express their sympathy with Mr Gladstone in his most painful position.'

DEBATE ON THE COERCION BILL

May 29th [1882]

Replying to Mr Gladstone, he said:

'As regards the Bill itself I will only say that I believe, to the fullest extent, in the good intentions of the Prime Minister, and of the Chief Secretary to the Lord Lieutenant. I believe they do not intend to use the Bill to injure the liberties of our people. I believe that they intend to use it only to put down crime in Ireland, but we have heard the same thing before now. We have heard the same words from the lips of every Minister of the Crown who since the Union has presented to this House a Coercion Bill for Ireland. I admit that perhaps the intentions of many of them were not the same as those of the right hon. gentleman, but Coercion Bills for Ireland have always been presented to this House with the same expression of a desire to preserve public and private liberty as those which have accompanied the presentation of this Bill on the present occasion . . . We do not believe that any man is good enough, or noble enough, to be entrusted with the liberties of a whole people. The two right hon. gentlemen who have spoken on this question have said that they do not intend to do this, and that they do not intend to do that, but that they wish to use the Bill in a certain way. I wish, however, to point out that the Bill leaves it absolutely in the power and in the discretion of the Executive Government, and the representatives of the Crown and the police to do what they please as regards supposed constitutional action, public or private, of any kind whatever. We say that going to Ireland with the best intentions you are going sooner or later bound to have them perverted or destroyed by the evil counsels which have reduced the right hon. member for Bradford (Mr Forster) to his present position. There is in Ireland an official circle, which represents but a very small minority of the people of the country, a class who are saturated with evil traditions, and it is utterly impossible that any man, no matter how strong he may be – no matter how imbued he may be with the principles of liberty – to resist the influences and avoid the action of that class for any considerable period. It therefore comes to this, that we are asked in this present Bill to surrender everything into the keeping of the Chief Secretary to the Lord Lieutenant. Now, sir, what does this Bill do? It gives the right to judges to try and sentence cases of treason, treason-felony, murder, firing at the person, manslaughter, and some other offences of a diverse and different character. In other words, it puts political offences and the most horrible crimes upon the same footing. I do not wish to deny for a moment that political offences are not carefully entitled to your consideration, and that you should obtain whatever guarantees you can, or may think proper, for their prevention; but I do deny that you are entitled to choose your judges and your executioners of the infliction of these sentences upon us out of the class who are our political opponents, and against whom we have been fighting in Ireland for the last two years. . . . I pass on to offences against the Act, and I must protest against the course which has been pursued by the framers of the Bill in reference to this part of it. Not only do you promise special tribunals, for the trial of offences which are already offences according to the ordinary law of the land, but you create special tribunals for trying them. You create the offence of constructive intimidation, and you make it of such a wide character that it is absolutely impossible for any person to do or say anything in Ireland, no matter what his intentions might be, without subjecting himself to the risk of being sent to prison for six months with hard labour . . .

Imprisonment with hard labour in the Irish prisons is little short of slavery . . . We have been contending against the right hon. gentleman (Mr Gladstone) for two years. We have found him to be a great and a strong man. I even think it is no dishonour to admit that we should not wish to be fought again in the same way by anybody in the future. I regret that the event in the Phoenix Park has prevented him continuing that course of conciliation which we had expected from him. I regret that, owing to the exigencies of his party and his position in the country he has felt himself compelled to turn from that course of conciliation and concession into the horrible paths of coercion which you have often had before, and in which your statesmen have always failed to reach what they set before them when they started, and which, I fear, on the present occasion, will lead to much greater disaster in the country than ever it led to before.'

During an interview with a *New York Herald* correspondent, Mr Parnell made the following remarks with reference to Mr Davitt's scheme of Land Nationalisation:

'In my judgment, however theoretically sound the plan for the nationalisation of the land may be considered in the opinion of its supporters, I cannot see how it can ever come in Ireland within the region of practical politics. The original programme of the Land League movement claimed for Irish tenants the right of becoming occupying owners, and cutting down of rents was to be the necessary preliminary to attaining this right. In using the expression, "The Land for the People", I never intended to convey my adhesion to nationalisation, but I meant that if Irish tenants were converted into occupying owners the land would be held in such a way, and cultivated in such a manner as to be of the most advantage to the whole of the people, because experience has shown that under this system it could and would be cultivated to the highest pitch, and made to produce the most food of which it is capable. The taxing power, which for purposes of freeing any other classes in the community from the burthen of taxation and throwing it upon the land, an Irish National Government might hereafter have under the plan of nationalisation, it would equally have under the Plan of occupying ownership, which, as I have said, originally constituted, has always been up to the present the programme of the Land League.'

DEBATE ON THE COERCION ACT

June 13th [1882]

'Mr Parnell did expect that the Government would have made some attempt to justify the powers they sought under this clause. They asked for the Irish police a protection which they did not claim for the policeman in the worst slums of London. In a city where 599 dead bodies had been found in the Thames during the last five years; where there were probably double that number of undetected murders, the Government did not claim for their police the power which it claimed for the Irish Stipendiary Magistrates with regard to infliction of sentences upon people who might assault the Irish police. . . .Why did the Government want this clause? Had the police been assaulted in Ireland? He asserted that assaults upon the police had been proportionately ten times greater in England. There had been comparatively no assaults upon the police in Ireland. The necessity, therefore, for the provisions of this Bill did not exist. Its provisions were calculated to make the Liberal Ministry and English rule hated for all eternity by the Irish people, if, indeed, eternal hatred had not been pro-voked by the measures of a similar character that had gone before it. Its provisions were calculated to keep the gap between the two nations wide apart . . .The Irish members could prove by the constitution and character of the police force, and by their actions, that they were not entitled to the extensive protection which the

Government desired to give them under this clause. It had not been shown that such a judicious use had been made of the very large powers of protection already given to the police by the law of the land as to entitle Parliament to give them further powers. During the last six months if anyone opened his mouth in Ireland, in a sense adverse to the present Government, he would do so at a risk of being picked up a few minutes later with a load of buckshot in him. If he whispered any thought which might appear to make out that everything the late Chief Secretary did was not perfection and most righteous, he ran the risk of finding a bayonet through his body before the words were well out of his mouth . . . The way the police were able to provoke the people was well known, and the additional powers asked for could not be justified either by the number or character of the assaults on the police.'

DEBATE ON THE COERCION BILL

June 15th [1882]

'Mr Parnell said it was a remarkable fact that whenever any abuse was to be heaped upon Irishmen there were Irishmen always found to do it with greater zest than appertained to any other nationality. He recollected when the member for Dublin University[18] heaped abuse in that House upon a most distinguished and honourable Irishman. He remembered when the right honourable gentleman justified his vote against the admission of Mr John Mitchel as member for Tipperary, on the ground that he was a dishonourable felon. No Englishman ventured to make such an allegation against Mr Mitchel. It was reserved for an Irishman, and he the member for Dublin University, to attempt to heap dishonour upon a man as honourable as himself. The right honourable gentleman looked forward with the highest exultation to the passage of this Bill into law, because when it was passed he and his class would have everything under their thumb in Ireland. They would be able to take up an attitude of hostility to the just claims of the Irish tenant farmers. That was what was really involved in this question. They knew that upon those unjust laws depended their power to claim unjust and exorbitant rents from the Irish tenant farmers . . . By this Bill they were about to subject the liberties and property of everybody in Ireland to the mercy of the servants of the Crown. They would find that with this Coercion Act they had made the greatest mistake . . . The impossibility of governing Ireland would grow daily, and so, perhaps, after all, the people of this country would come to agree with them that it would be better for the Irish people to govern themselves.'

DEBATE ON THE COERCION ACT

June 29th [1882]

'Mr Parnell thought they had every reason to complain that the conduct of this very important Bill, touching, as it might, the Irish people during every moment of their lives, and depriving them of every constitutional right, had been left to a member of the Ministry (Sir William Harcourt) who had no practical acquaintance with the government of Ireland other than that which he had received from his informants in the Home Office . . . He (Mr Parnell) had practical experience for the last eight sessions, and never during that time had he known of a Bill where concessions had been so stubbornly resisted by the Minister in charge, and where concessions which might have been reasonably granted, small concessions had been refused. This was a matter which, perhaps, affected the means of existence of a great many people in Ireland . . . The Home Secretary was acting under the influence of absurd panic in this matter. He said that he and the late Chief Secretary, the member for Bradford, were the two curses of the administration. To the false information supplied by the Home Office in London and the Castle in Dublin, by men who ought to be treated as cast-off hacks by a respectable and justice-loving Irish Administration, was due the way in which the Act of last year had been administered.'

August 16th [1882]

After the Freedom of Dublin City was conferred on Mr Parnell in the City Hall, he made the following remarks:

'I had intimated to your lordship (Mr Charles Dawson, Lord Mayor of the city at the time) in private that in view of the present state of the law of this country, and also of the administration of that law, for all practical purposes freedom of speech in my judgment has ceased to exist, and I had suggested to your lordship that I might be permitted to sign this roll conferring upon me this great and signal honour in private. But the matter has been ruled otherwise, and we are now assembled together, and I merely alluded to my opinion with regard to the cessation of freedom of speech in order to make you understand that I do not speak freely to day; that I shall not venture to touch upon matters of general politics, for as I have already said, I could not trespass into these domains without breaking the law of the land . . . I am sorry to say that I recognise to-day a situation in Ireland and an action by the Executive authorities in this country which does not propose to leave even the members of this ancient corporation the right of expressing their thoughts and opinions with regard to matters of public policy . . . I have spoken my mind in times past in this country, and I am vain enough to think that the expression of some of the sentiments to which I gave utterance has been attended with beneficial results to my country. I believe that we have gained some things for Ireland; but I also believe that Ireland has gained much more for herself by the independent action of the people of this country, the knowledge they have acquired of their rights, and their determination to use those rights. Much of what has been gained during the last year, I say is due to the independent action of the people of this country . . . I do not wish to attach too much importance to what can be gained by the action of your members in the House of Commons. Much good has resulted, and much good will result from an independent Parliamentary representation, but I have never claimed for Parliamentary action anything more than its just share of weight . . . I have never believed in the possibility of maintaining an independent Irish Party in the House of Commons for any length of time, but I believe it is possible to increase its numbers and to maintain it for such a time as will enable us to gain the great object of reform which has always possessed the hearts of the Irish people at home and abroad. I mean the restoration of the legislative independence of Ireland.'

Speaking at the Irish Labourers' League, 21st August [1882], he said – 'During the discussions on the Land Act of last year, and during the proceedings of the Convention, I pointed out that in my judgment the labourer ought to be independent of his employer so far as his house and little plot of ground were concerned, and that no mere tenure of half an acre of land from his immediate employer could be deemed to be a satisfactory solution or anything more than an attempt at a temporary solution of the labour difficulty . . . I think still that we shall not have a satisfactory settlement of this pressing difficulty until we have local authorities of a representative character, in the election of whom the labourers would share, who would have the power to take possession compulsorily of land in suitable situations for the benefit of the labouring classes. In this way the labourers would be independent of their employers – the farmers – so far as the roof over their head and the plot of land necessary to grow vegetables for their families would go. I should also hope that by extending that principle of compulsory purchase of land we might be able to deal even in a more extensive manner with the question of the labourers, but in the meanwhile I would earnestly exhort both classes, labourers and farmers, to be mutually tolerant of each other. To the farmers I would say – give to the labourers the half acre of ground they are asking from you; and to the labourers I would say – do not push your claims beyond the bounds of prudence and moderation, and do not advocate those claims in any way which would be considered contrary to the law of the land, or in any way which would be objectionable in its spirit or in its manner to the farmers from whom you are asking those concessions. Then, after a time, I should hope that we would obtain further legislation which would enable us to make the condition of the labouring classes very much more tolerable, and very much more what it should be in a Christian country.'

At the public meeting held in the Ancient Concert Rooms, Dublin, to establish the Irish National League, 17th October [1882], Mr Parnell presided. In the course of his speech he said: 'The proposed constitution of our organization may be said to comprise five leading features – first, national self government; secondly, land law reform; thirdly, local self government; fourthly, extension of the Parliamentary and municipal franchise; and fifthly, the development and encouragement of the labour and industrial interests of Ireland. It is proposed that the name of the organization shall be the Irish National League . . . I wish to affirm the opinion which I have expressed ever since I first stood upon an Irish platform – that until we obtain for the majority of the people of this country the right of making their own laws, we shall never be able, and we never can hope, to see the laws of Ireland in accordance with the wishes of the people of Ireland, or calculated, as they should, to bring about the permanent prosperity of our country. And I would always desire to impress upon my fellow-countrymen that their first duty, and their first object is to obtain for our country the right of making her own laws upon Irish soil . . . I wish to re-affirm the belief which I have expressed upon every platform upon which I have stood since the commencement of the land agitation – that no solution of the land question can be accepted as a final one that does not insure to the occupying farmers the right of becoming owners by purchase of the holdings which they now occupy as tenants . . . No measure of land reform, in my judgment, can ever be complete or satisfactory – can ever terminate the strife between the two classes – landlords and tenants – which has unhappily existed for centuries, which does not put the tenant farmer and his improvements beyond the reach of the chicanery of the law by making him the owner of his own holding.'

DEBATE ON THE CLOTURE

House of Commons
November 14th [1882]

Mr Parnell said – 'I would wish to impress upon the Irish constituencies the lesson that the Prime Minister spoke to them this evening when he pointed out that it would be always in their power by returning forty members to sit on these benches to obtain a discussion at the proper time on any Irish question of urgent public importance.'

DEBATE ON PROCEDURE

November 30th [1882]

'It has been said that Irish questions have lately taken up an undue portion of the time of the Legislature. As I said a while ago it was not our fault, and it was very much against our wishes that certain of these questions, such as the Coercion Acts, have taken up so much time . . . We have been told that very probably but little time would be given for Irish legislation during the remainder of this Parliament. I don't know how this may be, but what I would wish to submit to the House is this – that you have undertaken to legislate for Ireland that you have inherited from former times the duties of attending to the legislative requirements of the Irish people, and so long as you insist upon the propositions that this House is capable and qualified to attend to the wants and wishes of Ireland, I say it rests upon this House, and it is absolutely essential that this House should take up and attend to these wishes and requirements – and in the absence of any other plan – and no other plan has been proposed by which you can attend to the wants of Ireland – I think we are entitled to ask the Government that they should give a careful consideration to the suggestions* which have been made by my hon. friend (F. H. O'Donnell), so that at least a field of usefulness and of activity may be afforded to the Irish members representing the counties and boroughs of Ireland upon questions in which they take a deep interest.'

AT CORK

December 17th [1882]

'I cannot be so vain as to suppose for a moment that any of the praise and any of this honour you have showered upon me is my due. I know rather that it is not on account of your estimate of my personal worth or ability that you thus assemble to greet me, but rather because you believe that I have held firm to these principles which I first pledged myself to on the plains of Royal Meath in

---

*This refers to Mr F. H. O'Donnell's amendment with regard to Standing Committees. He proposed that after Irish Bills dealing with law or with trade had passed through the double ordeal of the first and second reading, they should be submitted for examination and investigation to a Standing Committee composed exclusively of Irish members.

1875, and afterwards renewed my pledges in this city to you in 1880. It is because you believe that I have done my best to help the suffering people of Ireland – because you think that I have held fast by the doctrine of independent opposition and of independence of both English political parties so long as these parties refuse to recognise the just rights of Ireland – the doctrines which were first practised by Lucas, Duffy and Dillon; doctrines which were enunciated by Joseph Ronayne[19] – doctrines which he taught to me, and which I laid before you at the last general election – it was because of your believing that I would faithfully carry out these pledges that you elected me, and I am proud to think to-day, that after my seven years of political service I can examine my heart and find that my mind is unchanged . . . I trust so long as life may be spared me I will still think and believe as you act, think and believe as you wish me to act, think and believe, and that I may always have the generous confidence and support in difficult times which you have never failed to give me.'

AT THE BANQUET THAT EVENING

'The question of National self-government is a question which is rapidly coming to the front. Both the English parties know well that the next general election in England will be turned by the votes of the Irish electors living in England upon that question. They tell us that no English ministry and no English member must ever entertain for a moment the idea of national self-government for Ireland. I believe that the time is rapidly approaching when they will have to entertain that idea, or some other idea which they may not like so well.'

DEBATE ON THE ADDRESS

House of Commons
February 23rd, 1883

{The Session of 1883 opened with a ferocious invective directed against Mr Parnell by the late Mr W. E. Forster. The Liberals and Tories applauded frantically the speech of the ex-Chief Secretary, to which Mr Parnell replied with cold scorn.}

'. . . I can assure the House that it is not my belief that anything I can say, or wish to say at this time, will have the slightest effect on the public opinion of the House, or upon the public opinion of this country. I have been accustomed during my political life to rely upon the public opinion of those whom I have desired to help, and with whose aid I have worked for the cause of prosperity and freedom in Ireland: and the utmost that I desire to do in the very few words which I shall address to this House, is to make my position clear to the Irish people at home and abroad from the unjust aspersions which have been cast upon me by a man who ought to be ashamed to devote his high ability to the task of traducing them. I don't wish to reply to the questions of the right hon. gentleman. I consider he has no right to question me, standing as he does in a position very little better than an informer with regard to the secrets of the men with whom he was associated, and he has not even the pretext of that remarkable informer (James Carey[20]) whose proceedings we have lately heard of. He had not even the pretext of that miserable man that he was attempting to save his own life. No, sir: other motives of less importance seem to have weighed with the right hon. gentleman in the extraordinary course which he has adopted on the present occasion of going out of his way to collect together a series of extracts, perhaps nine or ten in number, out of a number of speeches – many hundreds and thousands – delivered during the Land League movement by other people and not by me, upon which to found an accusation against me for what has been said and done by others . . . the right hon. gentleman has asked me to defend myself. Sir, I have nothing to defend myself for. The right hon. gentleman has confessed that he attempted to obtain a declaration or public promise from me which would have the effect of discrediting me with the Irish people. He has admitted that he failed in that attempt, and failing in that attempt, he lost his own reputation. He boasted last night that he had deposed me from some imaginary position which he was pleased to assign to me; but, at least, I have this consolation – that he also deposed himself . . . I have taken very little part in Irish politics since my release from Kilmainham. I expressed my reason for that upon the passing of the Crimes Act. I said that, in my judgment, the Crimes Act would result in such a state of affairs that between the Government and secret societies it would be impossible for constitutional agitation to exist in Ireland. I believe so still . . . It would have been far better if you were going to pass an Act of this kind and to administer an Act of this kind as you are going to administer it, and as you are obliged to administer it – up to the hilt – that it should be done by the seasoned politician who is now in disgrace. Call him back to his post! Send him to help Lord Spencer in his congenial work of the gallows in Ireland! Send him to look after the Secret Inquisitions of Dublin Castle! Send him to superintend the payment of blood money! Send him to distribute the taxes which an unfortunate and starving peasantry have to pay for crimes not committed by them! All this would be congenial work. We invite you to man your ranks, and send your ablest and best men. Push forward the task of misgoverning Ireland! For my part I am confident as to the future of Ireland. Although her horizon may appear at this moment clouded, I believe that our people will survive the present oppression as we have survived many and worse ones. And although our progress may be slow it will be sure, and the time will come when this house and the people of this country will admit once again that they have been mistaken; that they have been deceived by those who ought to be ashamed of deceiving them that they have been led astray as to the method of governing a noble, a generous, and an impulsive people; that they will reject their present leaders who are conducting them into the terrible course, which, I am sorry to say, the Government appears to be determined to enter; that they will reject these guides and leaders with just as much determination as they rejected the services of the right hon. gentleman the member for Bradford.'

DEBATE ON THE ADDRESS — THE CRIMES ACT

February 26th [1883]

'The Irish people have an earnest longing for fair play. They desire nothing but fair play: but when they see juries packed in the way described, and judges jumping about on the Bench when delivering their judgments, making themselves practically Crown prosecutors; when they see these things done while prisoners are on trial for their lives, then I say the inevitable result is to destroy all sympathy of the people for law and order, and to make the people endeavour to shield criminals. It could have no other effect. The worst traditions of Ireland are associated with this question of jury-packing and this question of the conduct of judges, and I regret to say that during the administration of the Crimes Act there have been more scandals than have ever occurred in the same time before. . .We have been taught by history that whenever we are orderly, whenever we obey the law, whenever a strong Coercion Act compels that respect and obedience to the law which the people do not feel, we receive no attention to our wants and necessities; but that when a great agitation arises which shakes the foundation of society, threatens revolution in civil war, we may expect that the undivided attention of the House of Commons may be given to the affairs of Ireland. . . . Nobody can deny that the situation and position of Ireland in the English constitutional system is one of the greatest importance, and that it will be impossible for the great Liberal party to continue its course of usefulness to England, the Empire, and I trust to the world at large, without the support and assistance – the cordial assistance – of Ireland. You never can have that assistance so long as you trample upon and oppress her people.'

DEBATE ON THE ADDRESS – DISTRESS IN IRELAND

March 1st [1883]

'We cannot help seeing that the Government of Ireland at the present moment is not a Government by Parliament, that it is not a Government by the Cabinet, but that it is a Government by Lord Spencer: and that nobleman seems to suppose that because he succeeded to the Government at an unusual time, he is entitled to depart from all constitutional precedents, and to rule Ireland as if she had not a representative system and as if, in fact, she was outside the pale of the Constitution and in the position of a conquered province. Such a system as that, if persevered in, must break down sooner or later. It cannot last . . . Lord Spencer has said that the people must go, and Lord Spencer being now all powerful will have his way at all events for, I sincerely hope, a very limited period.'

DEBATE ON THE TREATMENT OF PRISONERS IN IRELAND

March 11th [1883]

'Mr Parnell said this was a question in which he had always been very much interested, and which he had specially studied from the first moment of his entrance into Parliamentary life, and it was with the greatest possible disappointment that he found the guarantees they had fought for and won from the Conservative party when they were in office had been filched from untried prisoners in Ireland by the Imperial Government. It would be impossible to allow this matter to pass by without drawing the attention of the House of Commons to it. . . . He had no means of knowing how many persons were in prison under the summary jurisdiction powers of the magistrates in Ireland, but he could well understand the amount of irritation and the vindictive feelings with which the man who had come out of prison was moved if he had been half starved by cold and hunger while in that prison for a political offence, and if he had been made to associate with and do the work of criminals. . . . It had always been one of the special stains on English prison treatment that they had never drawn a distinction between the political offender and the person who had committed ordinary crime. The laws of France, Germany, and even Russia drew this distinction, but until the Act of 1877 was passed, in which the Irish members obtained the insertion of special powers for the treatment of prisoners convicted of sedition and seditious libel there never had been any attempt made in the Statute Books of England to give special treatment by law, though political prisoners had often experienced the benefit of the special interference of the authorities.'

DEBATE ON THE AMENDMENT OF THE LAND ACT

March 14th [1883]

'It is useless for the Government to live in a fool's paradise, and to shout out that the Irish land question is settled for ever. The Irish land question is not settled, and I feel convinced that it never can be settled until the chief provisions of the Bill which I now propose have been made the law of the land. Until the tenant's improvements are protected beyond yea or nay, until he is certain that the labour and capital which he invested in the soil will be his, and that no legal quibble and no exertions on the part of the long robed gentlemen, whether they sit on the Bench or occupy the humbler position of advocates for the landlords, will be able to deprive him of the result of that labour and toil, you will not have the Irish land question settled.'

DEBATE ON THE LABOURERS (IRELAND) BILL

May 30th [1883]

Mr Parnell declared 'he had always felt it would be of great importance to give the labourer a house to live in and a garden plot apart from the immediate influence of his employer. He thought that every person who sold his labour was entitled to have a house to dwell in, and that he should not be compelled to look for shelter for himself and his family to the success of an agreement with his employer, who had an unfair advantage over the labourer, when a dispute as to wages or any other subject could result in the loss of shelter to the labourer and his family. So far as a rooftree and a small plot of ground went, the Government ought to place the labourer in an independent position. That was the principle taken up in the Artisans' Dwellings Act, They now asked that that principle which had been worked out successfully by corporations in towns of 25,000 inhabitants and upwards should be extended to rural authorities who governed much larger numbers of people.'

AT CLONES – DURING MONAGHAN ELECTION CONTEST

June 20th [1883]

'Don't suppose that because the constitutional rights of public meetings and of public agitation are limited that therefore your cause can be thrown back. Hold the ground you have obtained, and press on for more . . . Select men who won't be afraid to stand by the side of the people and take their share of whatever peril and danger they ask the people to undergo.'

AT CARRICKMACROSS

June 29th [1883]

'Although the Land Act (of 1881) was maimed and mutilated in its passage to such an extent as to render this new effort on your part necessary, yet it was not the fault of the people of Ireland that you did not then obtain that full and complete justice for which we have yet to struggle. It was because the nation of Ireland was held down and trampled upon by a stronger and more powerful nation that the unequalled exertions of her people only proved partially availing, but depend upon it the march of your nation to your rights cannot be continually resisted. Although for a moment our enemies have proved stronger, depend upon it that yours is the cause which will grow in strength, which will increase and flourish, and be vigorous when the coercion laws under which we live shall be as dead and rotten as the authors of them.'

AT THE BANQUET GIVEN BY THE LORD MAYOR OF DUBLIN TO SENATOR JONES

June 30th [1883]

{Senator Jones, of Florida, USA who was entertained at a banquet on this occasion, had during the land agitation rendered conspicuous services to the Irish cause in America. At this time the United States Government had refused to permit pauper emigrants deported by the Castle from 'Congested Districts' of the West to be landed on American soil.}

'The English Government and English opinion are in many respects very amenable to the influences of public sentiment all over the world upon any question, even on the Irish question. We have lately had a signal example in reference to the emigration question of how susceptible English public opinion is to what is thought of them in other countries. This is a very proper feeling, and I do not suppose that I shall be accused of attempting to insult the British lion or committing any very heinous offence if I attribute to the English people that susceptibility, which undoubtedly attaches to them in an unusual degree. I trust that one of the results of what is passing in New York at the present moment* may be that the Government of this country may turn their attention to some practical way of utilising the bone and sinew which they are emigrating to New York – of utilising that bone and sinew at home instead of pursuing that suicidal and ridiculous course of emigrating a labouring population of the utmost importance for the development of our industrial resources at home to a country where they are better fed, though they cannot be possibly more wanting.'

BANQUET AT THE OPENING OF THE
CORK INDUSTRIAL EXHIBITION.

July 4th [1883]

'We can at all events create a native market here, and I believe also in America a market of Irish manufactures, and in this way taking advantage of the good will which throughout Ireland has been rendered evident on behalf of the restoration of Irish industries we can do much to revive the ancient fame of our nation in these

---

* This has reference to the action of the Government of the United States, in returning to Ireland pauper emigrants, sent out under the organization of Mr Tuke and the Liberal Government.

matters, which have rendered great those nations by the side of which we live. I trust that before many years are gone by we shall have the pleasure of meeting in even more places than this, and see that the quick-witted genius of the Irish race has proved what this great place has taught – a lesson which I hope will lead to our nation's happiness, prosperity, and freedom.'

DEBATE ON LAND COMMISSION VOTE

August 16th [1883]

'The law in Ireland for keeping down the people has been administered sternly and swiftly, but the Land Act, as has been plainly proved, has been administered tardily and inefficiently.'

DEBATE ON THE APPROPRIATION BILL –
THE CROSSMAGLEN CASES

August 23rd [1883]

'This case of the peasants convicted at the Belfast Assizes of conspiracy to murder has excited a very great amount of attention not only in the north of Ireland, but throughout the rest of the country, and he thought he was safe in saying that it was the universal conviction in Ireland, and that that conviction would still remain despite the eloquence of the Attorney-General for Ireland, that in the case in question a number of innocent persons were now enduring penal servitude: the belief was universal that these people were unjustly convicted and sentenced for offences which they had not committed . . . The learned gentleman said these prisoners were tried before a common jury. Yes, a jury of common Orange rowdies, taken from such localities as The Pound, and a class from which those ship carpenters come, who annually assembled armed with bludgeons and weapons for the purpose of attempting to take the lives of, or inflicting injury upon their Catholic fellow-countrymen. A special jury in Belfast would be infinitely less unfair in a trial of this kind than a common jury taken from that class. Their contention simply was that a jury of Northern Protestants taken from the class to which this common jury belonged could not possibly be a fair one under the circumstances . . . Would any hon. member like to be tried in any case, however slight, by a jury of illiterate men consisting of his political enemies . . . Yet these proceedings were of daily occurrence in Ireland, and had occurred in reference to the lives and liberties not of people of importance in the country, but of the humblest classes of mountain peasant, who were now suffering terrible sentences in Mountjoy prison . . .'

THE PARNELL NATIONAL TRIBUTE

December 11th [1883]

{One of the most representative gatherings ever held in Ireland, was the banquet in the Rotunda, at which Mr Parnell was presented with the National tribute. His speech on the occasion was a typical one, and transformed the gathering from a personal tribute to himself into an historical event, which those who had the good luck to be present can never forget.}

'My Lord Mayor, ladies and gentlemen, I do not know how adequately to express my feelings with regard not only to your lordship's address, not only to the address of the Parnell National Tribute, but also regarding this magnificent demonstration, for I can call it nothing else. But, my lord, I prefer to leave to the historian the description of to-night and the expression of an opinion as regards the results which to-night must produce. You, my lord, have recalled to our memories the historical occasion of the assemblage one hundred years ago in this hall. I trust that those who come after us – I not only trust, but I feel sure that those who come after us at the centennial anniversary of to-day will occupy a brighter, a higher, and a greater position, and will see their country occupy a greater and a higher position than we are fated to see to-day. I shall not attempt to reply in any way to your lordship's eulogy speaking as an Irishman to an assembly of Irishmen and Irish women. I shall only say that I believe, and I think that the result of the great movement of the last few years shows that I am right in that belief, that there must have been Irishmen who thought and felt as I did, many, undoubtedly, more able and more willing than I to give effect to my thoughts and my wishes. As an Irishman, I have no doubt in common with many thousands of my countrymen, I looked around me: I saw the artisan in the towns struggling for a precarious existence, with a torpid trade, with everything against him: I saw the Irish tenant farmer trembling before the eye of his landlord, with the knowledge that in that landlord's power rested the whole of the future of himself and of his family: that his position was literally no better, physically not so good as the lot of a South African negro: that he was endeavouring to make both ends meet, that his life was a constant struggle to keep the roof over his head and over the heads of his family by the most grinding and pinching self-denial. I saw, as you have all seen, the Irish labourer, whose lot even to this day has been but very little improved, and for whom there is now also I trust a ray of light and hope dawning. I saw the Irish labourer the lowest of the low, the slave of the slave, with not even a dry roof over his head, with the rain from heaven dripping upon the couch on which he was forced to lie: dressed with rags: subsisting on the meanest food: and whether I looked upon one side of the social system or upon the other side, irresistible conviction was borne back upon me that here was a nation carrying on its life, striving for existence, striving for nationhood under such difficulties as had never beset any other people on the face of Europe. Many of us saw these things. To many of us the same thoughts occurred. And some years ago we resolved – and I am proud and happy to say that at this board to-night there are many present who joined in that resolve – that these things should no longer be if we could help it. And the historian of the future will say for the Land League movement, if he be unprejudiced and faithful, that never was there such an infamous and horrible system – a system which even the British Parliament and the influence and laws of England have already partially admitted to be a gigantic system of robbery and fraud – that never was there a movement formed to contend against such a system with so much odds against it, in the carrying out of which I will not even say in connection with which, but in association with which there was so much moderation and discretion and such an utter absence of crime and of the strong passions which agitate men. (Cheers, in which the closing words of the sentence were lost.) . . . We always have to take into account that no matter how we may strive to keep within the limits of the Constitution, this strong people outside of us and practically opposed to us, will always meet us with the rule of force . . . and in striving for and obtaining the partial justice that we have yet obtained, we have been met with this rule of force. . . . In face of the fact that no man's life, much less his liberty, is at the present moment safe, Lord Hartington has the coolness to tell us that the Liberal Party will co-operate with the Irish Party when we abandon our unconstitutional ways, and use only constitutional methods. I would rather have preferred to say that until the Liberal Party abandon their unconstitutional methods and betake themselves to the observance of the British Constitution, there can be no co-operation between English Liberals and Irishmen in respect of those matters connected with the advancement of popular liberties and the progress of general reform to which such co-operation would be fairly permissible under normal conditions. . . . To enable such co-operation as would be consistent and permissible with our present position as an independent Irish Party, there must be no more coercion and no more emigration. We regard any system of emigration which has yet been tried in this country as a murderous blow against the life of our nation, accompanied by untold suffering to the unhappy individuals on whom the experiment is made . . . We have reason to be proud, hopeful, and energetic, determined that this generation shall not pass away until it has bequeathed to those who come after us the great birthright of National independence and prosperity.'

THE REFORM BILL

House of Commons
March 3rd, 1884

'The right hon. gentleman the member for Westminster (Mr W. H. Smith) when enumerating the disadvantages likely to arise if Ireland were included in the present Bill, spoke of the unfortunate habit belonging to Governments of being desirous of remaining in office, but he forgot to include also the unfortunate habit which belongs to Oppositions, of being desirous to come into office. When listening to the speech of the right hon. gentleman I thought I was listening to a speech delivered against a proposition for repealing the Union and for establishing our Irish Parliament, or one delivered in support of a proposition for disenfranchising Ireland altogether . . . I cannot understand the position of the right hon. gentleman, who has frequently asked this House to look upon Ireland as if she was so much a part of the United Kingdom as Yorkshire, that while not opposing, or not strongly opposing the extension of the suffrage in the counties of England, he should at the same time vehemently declare that the end of all things would come if the same measure of justice meted out to England and Scotland should be meted out to Ireland. One would think that the result of the inclusion of Ireland would be that in future laws would be made for Ireland by the members from Ireland . . . If you are to govern Ireland constitutionally under a representative system – if you are still going to permit her members to come here, you cannot with the smallest scrap of self-respect deny her the same franchise which you claim for this country. For my part, I believe that the interests with which we who sit upon these benches have been prominently identified during the last few years will survive even such injustice as that . . . Whether we be included in the Bill or whether we be not, we feel confident that the justice of our cause and the devotion of our people will enable us to carry the principles for which we stand together.'

DEBATE ON THE POLICE TAX – CAPTAIN PLUNKETT

March 16th [1884]

'The city of Cork, which I have the honour to represent, was distinguished during the whole of the great agrarian movement which resulted in the passage of the Land Act, by its entire absence from agrarian or political crime of any kind, and that state of affairs has continued to exist up to the present moment. During the last four years and for a number of years previous there has been an entire absence of agrarian or political crime of any kind in the city of Cork, and it is a city such as this that the satellites of the Irish Government choose for the practice of deeds which have not been paralleled in any part of Ireland. They have inflicted on the citizens of Cork an extra police tax, which since it was first inflicted amounts to the enormous sum of £15,000. They have held secret inquiries and they have hauled respectable citizens entirely innocent of any crime before the magistrates, and sent them to prison because they were unable to give any information. They have endeavoured to blacken the fame of individual politicians, not because these persons would [not] give them any information about anything, but because their general political course had made them obnoxious to magnates such as Captain Plunkett,[21] and when at last all parties in Cork united together and asked that those extra police might be removed, they got a reply from the Chief Secretary (Mr Trevelyan) which I do not wish to characterise as shuffling, but which entirely evaded the point put forward, and leaves the subject in a most unsatisfactory state . . . The Corporation of Cork in reference to this matter have determined that they won't pay the tax, and the Corporation of Limerick have followed their example. Now, does the right hon. gentleman ever consider what would be the result of a general strike in Ireland, not against paying rent, but against the payment of this police tax? Has he ever considered whether the difficulty of his administration would not be enormously increased if the ratepayers who are being mulcted for a number of years for the cost of extra police in different counties in Ireland were to say, ' We won't pay this tax, but we will allow you to collect it'? . . . I believe that the resistance of this payment for extra police and for blood money would be just as successful as the resistance to tithes in 1832 and 1833 . . . The right hon. gentleman has endeavoured to trade upon the Invincible conspiracy, and to represent in his speeches that the whole of Ireland was seething in one vast conspiracy, instead of insisting that his officials throughout Ireland should learn to govern the country without reliance upon exceptional methods so as to prepare for a return of the time when they would have to do without them – a time which is very fast approaching. . . . Recourse to coercion is like recourse to opium – the more you have the more you want.'

ST PATRICK'S DAY CELEBRATION – BANQUET IN LONDON

[1884]

'I do not depend upon any English political party. I should advise you not to depend upon any such party. I do not depend upon the good wishes of any section of the English people. Although Ireland may have friends amongst Englishmen, and undoubtedly has many friends amongst Englishmen, yet the circumstances of Ireland's position, the nature of her case, render it impossible for them, however well disposed, to give that effectual assistance and work which are absolutely necessary to obtain the welfare of our country. Some people desire to rely on the English democracy – they look for a great future movement amongst the English democracy, but I have never known any important section of any country which has assumed the governing of another country to awaken to the real necessities of the position until compelled to do so. A spirit has been infused amongst our people which will never die.'

AT DROGHEDA

April 15th [1884]

{This speech was delivered in answer to a pronouncement by Mr Davitt condemning the individual ownership of land, and advocating nationalization on the lines of Mr Henry George's plan. Mr Davitt was assailed fiercely by the very men who, a year ago, joined him in hounding down Mr Parnell – notably by Mr T. P. O'Connor in the columns of the New York *Sun* and other journals.}

'Four years ago the people of Ireland, that is such of them as were entrusted with the vote, returned at a very short notice, and in the face of very great difficulties of every kind, returned for the first time to Parliament, an independent, united party, pledged to keep aloof from both the English parties, and for four sessions that party for the first time in the history of Parliamentary relations between England and Ireland has kept its pledges, has remained unbroken, has continually added to its strength, its discipline, and its knowledge, and has constantly extracted from its enemies testimony of its worth and power . . . It is necessary for me to take advantage of this occasion to warn you against elements of future difficulty – elements of possible future difficulty and possibilities of grave disunion in our ranks, which may be obviated by my timely declaration. I refer to the project termed the nationalisation of the land, and in dealing with this question I don't wish to intrude upon you anything of a personal character. I prefer, as I always have done in public life and history, to deal with principles and not with men. I have read for you the two planks of the platform of the Land League – the destruction of rack rents and of landlord oppression and evictions, and the facilitation of occupying ownership by the tiller of the soil. Well, unmindful of this fact we have been recently informed upon distinguished authority at a meeting in Dublin that we have been false to the spirit of the Land League, that we are unmindful of its principles, because we refused to desert that which has been our programme up to the present moment and follow this new craze. Ownership of land by anybody, we are told, is theft. Whether that anybody be landlord or tenant it is equally a crime and a robbery, and because we refuse to agree with the sweeping assertion we are condemned as slack and as yielding basely to the present Coercion Act. The desire to acquire land is everywhere one of the strongest instincts of human nature, and never more developed than in a country such as Ireland, where land is limited and those who desire to acquire it are numerous. I submit further, that this desire to acquire landed property, and the further desire to be released from the crushing impositions of rack rents, was the very basis and foundation of the National Land League, and that without it, although not solely owing to it, we never could have progressed or been successful. As reasonably might we have supposed that we could have persuaded the poor man that it was with him a crime to endeavour to hope for the ownership of the holding he tilled. No more absurd or preposterous proposition was ever made to a people than, after having declared on a thousand platforms by a million voices that the tenant should be the owner of his holding – that after this declaration had been agreed to by a million of our own countrymen in England, America, and Australia – after having, with unexampled success, proceeded forward on these lines for five years, we should quietly turn round, retrace our steps to the starting post, and commence anew a movement which should be wanting in every element and prospect of success, and of the successful working of which even its supporters could not afford us any single example . . . I have neither advanced nor receded, from the position which I took up in 1879. It was a position which I thought you would be able to carry, and which in all probability you will be able to carry. . . . I said in New York, in 1879, when I landed there, what I say to you to night – that you must either pay for the land or fight for it . . . Constitutional agitation and organization can do a great deal to whittle down the price that the landlord asks for his land, but it must be paid unless you adopt the other alternative which I say nothing about. We are told of some great wave of English democracy which is coming over here to poor Ireland to assist the Irish democracy. The poor Irish democracy will have, I fear, to rely upon themselves in the future as they have had to do up to the present moment . . . The land question of Ireland must be settled by the Irish people at home. We have a people who in the face of every discouragement and disadvantage have gradually forced their way up until their attitude has come to be regarded by both friend and foe alike as sound. Their position is impregnable. If you have progressed with a limited suffrage, and in the face of the worst Coercion Acts ever inflicted upon a country, what will you do when coercion has been blotted out, and when you have the security which will enable you to press on for the liberty and security of our country?'

AT TIPPERARY

January 8th, 1885

{At the Tipperary Convention in Thurles, held on this date, some difficulty arose owing to the desire of a section of the delegates to adopt a local gentleman instead of Mr John O'Connor of Cork, who was recommended by Mr Parnell.}

'If division should arise amongst us, either amongst the people or their leaders, the day of regeneration may be deferred although it cannot be indefinitely postponed.'

AT CORK

January 21st [1885]

'I hold that it is better even to encourage you to do what is beyond your strength, even should you fail sometimes in the attempt, than to teach you to be subservient and unreliant . . . We consider that whatever class tries to obstruct the labourer in the possession of those fair and just rights to which he is entitled that class shall be put down – and coerced if you will – into doing justice to the labourer . . . It is given to none of us to forecast the future, and just as it is impossible for us to say in what way or by what means the National question may be settled – in what way full justice may be done to Ireland – so it is impossible for us to say to what extent that justice should be done. We cannot ask for less than the restitution of Grattan's Parliament, with its important privileges, and wide and far-reaching constitution. We cannot, under the British

Constitution, ask for more than the restitution of Grattan's Parliament, but no man has a right to fix the boundary of the march of a nation. No man has a right to say 'Thus far shalt thou go, and no further;' and we have never attempted to fix the *ne plus ultra* to the progress of Ireland's nationhood, and we never shall. But, gentlemen, while we leave these things to time, circumstances, and the future, we must each one of us resolve in our own hearts that we shall at all times do everything that within us lies to obtain for Ireland the fullest measure of her rights. In this way we shall avoid difficulties and contentions amongst each other. In this way we shall not give up anything which the future may put in favour of our country: and while we struggle to-day for that which may seem possible for us without combination, we must struggle for it with the proud consciousness that we shall not do anything to hinder or prevent better men who may come after us from gaining better things than those for which we now contend.'

AT ENNIS

January 25th [1885]

Alluding to Mr Lysaght Finnegan's election in 1879, Mr Parnell said:

'I have always found that Ennis has been true and faithful, and this magnificent demonstration, originating spontaneously, without preparation, from your hearts, shows that you are to-day what you were then. It was no ordinary help you gave me in 1879. That was a turning point in my history, and in the history of Ireland also.'

ST PATRICK'S DAY BANQUET IN LONDON

[1885]

'Ireland a nation! Ireland has been a nation: she is a nation; and she shall be a nation. England will respect you in proportion as you and we respect ourselves. They will not give anything to Ireland out of justice or righteousness. They will concede you your liberties and your rights when they must and no sooner . . . We can none of us do more than strive for that which may seem attainable to-day; but we ought at the same time to recollect that we should not impede or hamper the march of our nation; and although our programme may be limited and small it should be such a one as shall not prevent hereafter the fullest realization of the hopes of Ireland; and we shall, at least if we keep this principle in mind, have this consolation, that while we may have done something to enable Ireland in some measure to retain her position as a nation, to strengthen her position as a nation, we shall have done nothing to hinder others who may come after us from taking up the work with perhaps greater strength, ability, power and advantages than we possess, and from pushing to that glorious and happy conclusion which is embodied in the words of the toast which I now ask you to drink – "Ireland a nation!"'

INTERVIEW WITH THE IRISH LEADER

In *United Ireland*, immediately after the resignation of the Liberal Cabinet.

'The result of a division is a consequence of the policy which the Irish Party has adopted during the last four years of this Parliament – to turn out the Government at any cost as a lesson for all future Governments with regard to the determination of the Irish People not to submit to unconstitutional government or coercion . . . As regards the action of the Irish Party during the rest of the session, the Tories cannot possibly undertake to carry a Coercion Bill, and if the Conservative party could not make the attempt we will be disposed to give the new Government a fair trial. We have never attacked the Government merely for the sake of attack. We have done so in self-defence, and to save our country from injury.'

DEBATE ON THE ADMINISTRATION OF THE CRIMES ACT

House of Commons
July 17th [1885]

'The late Government had their own reasons for denying justice. I do not wish to throw water on a drowned rat; I do not wish to speak too harshly or too unkindly of the present occupants (the Liberals) of the front Opposition bench; but certainly they did all they possibly could to take over the guilt for the crime of others, if it be possible by denial of justice and by screening the offenders, to share in the responsibility in reference to crime and offences committed by others. Then I say that some of the guilt for the judicial murder of Myles Joyce[22] and for the imprisonment of four other innocent men rests with the present occupants of the front Opposition bench. We brought this case forward, and appealed for inquiry while they were in office, but I suppose that they considered that as they had done so much to outrage public feeling and public opinion in Ireland, they might do a little more. I am thankful for the turn of events and what I believe to be retributive justice, and I am now able to indict before another tribunal the offences of the late Government against justice in Ireland. It may be possible for the Irish people to forgive the conduct of Lord Spencer, but I feel sure they will never forget it.'

AT ARKLOW

August 20th [1885]

'The life of Ireland is dependent upon her bone and sinew. Our population has diminished at the rate of a million a decade during the last 40 years; it is time that that should be put a stop to, and that it should be possible for the labourers, the artisans, and the mechanics of Ireland to live, thrive, and prosper at home.'

BANQUET GIVEN BY THE IRISH MEMBERS TO THEIR LEADER AT THE IMPERIAL HOTEL, DUBLIN

August 24th [1885]

'I say that each and all of us have only looked upon the Acts – the legislative enactments which we have been able to wring from an unwilling Parliament – as means towards an end, that we would have at any time, in the hours of our deepest depression and greatest discouragement, that we would have spurned and rejected any measure however tempting and however apparent for the benefit of our people, if we had been able to detect that behind it lurked any danger to the legislative independence of our land ... It is admitted by all parties that you have brought the question of Irish legislative independence to the point of solution. It is not now a question of self-government for Ireland; it is only a question as to how much of the self-government they will be able to cheat us out of. It is not now a question of whether the Irish people shall decide their own destinies and their own future, but it is a question with, I was going to say, our English masters – but we cannot call them masters in Ireland – it is a question with them as to how far the day, that they consider the evil day, shall be deferred. You are, therefore, entitled to say that so far you have done well, you have almost done miraculously well, and we hand to our successors an unsullied flag, a battle more than half won, and a brilliant history . . . Undoubtedly upon the choice of our future colleagues and their future action will, in all human probability, depend without exaggeration the future of Ireland and the fate of the nation – at all events in our time . . . We shall require undoubtedly in the new men of the Irish party the best ability, the sturdiest honesty and inflexibility, the truest judgment, and the most absolute self-negation that the country can supply . . . I hope that it may not be necessary for us in the new Parliament to devote our attention to subsidiary measures, and that it may be possible for us to have a programme and a platform with only one plank, and that one plank National Independence . . . May the next party contain, if possible, still greater elements of energy and sagacity, honesty and courage, than that which fought through the epoch which has just expired. May I find colleagues so generous to their leader and so loyal to each other . . . But it is undoubtedly upon our people at home that the main burden rests. It is they and they alone who can defeat the Irish cause. If they maintain the fixity of purpose and the union of the last five years no power on earth can resist them.'

AT THE MEETING OF THE NATIONAL LEAGUE

August 25th [1885]

'I believe that we will get a settlement of the National question from whichever Government or whichever party may be in power, whether it be Whig or whether it be Tory. There might be slight variations in the terms which we may succeed in securing from the one body or the other, but I believe that the settlement which we shall be able to obtain from the Tories will be as valuable and as important for the interests of Ireland and for the prosperity of the nation as the settlement that we shall be able to obtain from the Whigs or Radicals. We are, therefore, in the position that no matter which of the English sides loses or which of them wins, we are bound to win . . . When we have restored to us our own Parliament it will be possible for you to discuss and thresh out every question. Every man of different idea[s] will then have a stage on which he will be able to exemplify and enlarge his views; but for the present solidity is necessary in our ranks. Our desire is to restore to you the power of making for yourself and working out your own destiny. When you have got that power I believe you will use it rightly and bravely, and that the Irish nation will prosper and be perpetual.'

AT A BANQUET IN THE MANSION HOUSE, DUBLIN

September 1st [1885]

Mr Parnell, in proposing the toast 'Ireland a nation,' said:

'It is one which recalls to our minds many recollections; recollections of great men, of a long and enduring struggle, of many sufferings on the part of our people, and of a survival to-day of what is an Irish Nation, the survival of a people who have forced upon an unwilling opponent recognition of an actual fact – that Ireland still lives . . . I desire now to express my fullest conviction that the Irish people are on the brink of victory in this struggle. There is nothing in the world, humanly speaking, that could prevent their success save immoderation on their own part.'

AT THE CONVENTION IN WICKLOW

October 5th [1885]

'It is admitted that the present system cannot go on, and what are you going to put in its place? My advice to English statesmen considering this question would be this: – Trust the Irish people altogether or trust them not at all . . . Whatever chance the English rulers may have of drawing to themselves the affection of the Irish people lies in destroying the abominable system of Legislative

Union between the two countries by conceding fully and freely to Ireland the right to manage her own affairs ... The condition of English power is more insecure and more unstable at the present than it has ever been.'

DEBATE ON THE ADDRESS – THE IRISH QUESTION

House of Commons
January 21st, 1886

'We have been spoken to to-night about the necessity of protecting the loyal minority. Well, sir, I was myself born a Protestant, I have lived a Protestant, and I hope to die a Protestant, and if in the future, after the concession of the Irish claims, any danger were to arise to my Protestant fellow-countrymen, I should be the first to stand up for that liberty of speech and that liberty of conscience, and liberty to live and thrive of every section of the community, whether they were Protestants or whether they were Catholics; and perhaps I may be a more effectual aid to them in times of real danger than some of those gentlemen who talk so loudly and boast so much. . . . If there were no land question there would be no opposition on the part of any influential section or community in Ireland to the concession of Home Rule ... When it comes to be a struggle on the one side between the Irish landlords – and it must come to it – aided by the Government, and on the other side the Irish tenants, whom we represent, and the Irish labourers, we have no doubt as to which side we shall cast our lot upon.'

AT GALWAY

February 10th [1886]

{At the General Election of 1885, Mr T. P. O'Connor was elected for Galway Borough and for the Scotland Division of Liverpool.

Electing to sit for the latter constituency, he vacated Galway. Mr Parnell was induced to support the candidature of Captain O'Shea, who had failed to capture the Exchange Division of Liverpool from the Tories. This was the signal for an outbreak of the mutinous spirit which had for some time been spreading in the section of the party now known as the 'Bantry Band'.}

'I have told you that I did not know of Mr Lynch's claims, and having recommended him (Captain O'Shea) in my position, I was bound not to recede one hair's breadth, one jot, but carry through that recommendation to the bitter end, and to test whether the people of Galway and the people of Ireland had confidence in me, which I believe they have, and which the result of this election will show that they have renewed. I have never led during eleven long years, since my entry into public life, I have never led the Irish people astray. I have never led them into any crooked path. I have never led the Irish party astray. When courage was required, when it was necessary for the interests of the nation, I have shown it; and when moderation was required, when moderation was necessary, and temperate judgement for the interests of the nation, I had courage to show it, and I never will lead the party or the nation astray until we have gained for you the right to lead and govern yourselves.'

AFTER THE DECLARATION OF THE POLL

February 11th [1886]

'I am confident that in the near future the men of Galway who have stood by me to-day will recognize, when we bring back to them in triumph the right to make their own laws, that they have not trusted to us in vain, and that the dark days when poverty and misery must brood over a city and a noble people like this will have ceased for ever, and that with the right of self-government we shall have the power to raise up our population from their deep depression and their terrible misery, and that not only shall we do that but we shall build up our nation by degrees until she takes the place among the other nations of the earth which Providence and the courage of her children have evidently destined her.'

DEBATE ON SUNDAY CLOSING

House of Commons
April 2nd [1886]

'I have always endeavoured to keep clear of this temperance question. I have never voted on it, because I think the question of the control of the liquor trade is a question, above all others, with which most suitably and properly an Irish Legislature ought to deal.'

April 8th [1886]

After Mr Gladstone's statement regarding his measure of Home Rule.

'I do not desire to go back over old quarrels. It generally happens that those who have been defeated in old quarrels like to refer to them. But I have nothing to retract. What I said then I say now – that there had been the execution and imprisonment of innocent men. I believed it then – and I believe it now – that innocent men had been executed . . . I will pass on to the consideration of the Bill. I should like to reserve a too positive expression of opinion until I have seen the measure, but still I think it is right that I should say something about its merits as they have been explained to us by the right honorable the member for Midlothian. Allow me to say, sir, that I think it will prove to be a happy and fortunate thing both for Ireland and England that there was one man living, an English statesman, with the great power and extraordinary ability of the honorable gentleman to lend his voice to poor hapless Ireland on this question . . . Whatever may be the date of the measure, I believe the cause of Irish autonomy will gain enormously in a way it never could have otherwise gained by the genius of the right honorable gentleman. I thank him, therefore, for the energy and the time he has devoted to this matter, and I believe sincerely in my heart that the result will be that the people of England will recognise, as the result of what he has done, that he has been to them, no less than to the people of Ireland, a National benefactor. But there are, undoubtedly, great faults and blots in the measure . . . The right honorable gentleman has had, I suppose, to shape his measure to meet the tremendous opposition worked against it; but there are several points it will be our duty, when the measure reaches its committee stage, to oppose very strongly and to press for serious modifications and amendment. . .The question of the Royal Irish Constabulary has been left in a most unsatisfactory state . . . It is unfair to ask us to pay for a force over which we shall have no control whatever . . . As regards the measure itself, the Prime Minister has truly said that it ought not to proceed unless it is cheerfully welcomed, not only by the Irish members but by the Irish people. I quite agree with that.'

DEBATE ON THE SECOND READING OF THE ARMS BILL

May 20th [1886]

'We complain, apart altogether from the general principle of the right to bear arms, we complain that Acts such as these have been injuriously and unfairly used in two different directions – they have been used in the first place to harass and annoy the Nationalists of Ireland . . . When I first entered the House of Commons the Arms Act was under discussion, and I felt humiliated at the feeling that came over me, that I, who had just come from my constituency, then full of hope that the right of making her own laws would shortly be restored to Ireland, and no other feeling, that I should find the House of Commons was only willing to pay attention to a Bill to disarm the people of Ireland . . . I admit there may be some reason why at present, and considering the condition of a portion of the country, the hands of the Government might be fortified by some such measure as this. But that reason is not one created by anything on the part of the Nationalists.'

AT PORTSMOUTH, AFTER THE DEFEAT OF
MR GLADSTONE'S HOME RULE BILL

June 25th [1886]

'It is, I believe, about the first time I have had the honour of addressing a mainly English audience. And I have been induced to do so now because I rely greatly upon the spirit of fair play among the English masses, and because the issues for my country are so great and so vital at the present moment – the issues which underlie this present struggle – that the Irishman who remains silent when it might be possible to do something to help his country would be more unworthy than tongue could describe . . . I have, in my career as a member of Parliament, never wittingly injured the cause of the English working man. I have done something to show my sympathy for the masses of the people of this country . . . Some years ago it was my privilege to strike with English members a successful blow in favour of the abolition of flogging in the army and navy. We were met then by the very same arguments as we are met with to-day, and from the same class of persons. It was said by the late Lord Beaconsfield that the integrity of the British Empire would be endangered if flogging were abolished, and he called a great meeting at one of the Ministerial offices in London, a great meeting of his supporters both in the Lords and Commons, for the purpose of exhorting them to stand shoulder to shoulder in defence of the British Empire against the abolition of flogging in the army . . . I have shown you that in some respects the Irish settlement proposed by Mr Gladstone does not give a Parliament, a Legislature with the powers possessed by Grattan's Parliament; but I have shown you on the other hand that as regards our own exclusively domestic business it gives larger powers, more important powers, more valuable powers for Ireland itself than was possessed by Grattan's, and therefore we think that this settlement proposed by Mr Gladstone will prove a more durable settlement than the restitution of the Grattan Parliament or the Repeal of the Union would prove . . . Imperial unity does not require or necessitate unity of Parliaments. Will you carry that away with you and remember it, because it is the keystone of our whole proceedings . . . I should say that Ireland would justly deserve to lose her privilege if she passed laws oppressive of the minority . . . So far as coercion was concerned it has not brought you any nearer to the end of the Irish question . . . One great fault in English coercion has been that no matter what your intentions have been when you have commenced coercion, you have never discriminated between political agitators and breakers of the law . . . Lord Carnarvon will not deny that he was as strong a Home Ruler as I was last August, and that when he went over to Ireland he became stronger and stronger every day he lived in that country. There is another thing he has not denied: he has not denied that he sought an interview with me in order to speak to me and consult with me about a Constitution for Ireland . . . Untold is the guilt of that man who, for party purposes, does not take advantage of the spirit which is abroad amongst the English to put the hand of the Irish into that of the English to close the strife of centuries – a strife that has been of no advantage to the people of either country; a strife that has only been for the benefit of the money-grabbing landlords; a strife that has impeded popular progress in England as well as in Ireland, and that must continue to impede it; a strife which is fanned for the purpose of cheating you out of your rights, and to divert the energies of the newly enfranchised masses of Great Britain from the redress of their grievances to the odious task of oppressing and keeping down the small sister country.'

AT PLYMOUTH[23]

June 27th [1886]

Referring to the question of the Protestant minority in Ireland, he said: 'They will get abundance of fair play, and they know it well enough; and if fair play were wanting on the part of the majority of Irishmen then I say it should be just and right, if Irishmen so far forgot the honour of their country and the public opinion of the world as to revert to the bigoted and sectarian oppression of the Middle Ages, then I say it would be just and right for Englishmen to step in and take away this great privilege which Irishmen would then be proved to have abused . . .

{Referring to the Carnarvon controversy.[24]}

It is a favourite device with politicians when they are accused of one thing to say not that they did not do it, but that they did something else.'

AT CARDIFF

June 28th [1886]

'In fact, you will find that when you have conceded to Ireland the right of self-government a great many troubles and dangers which appear to you now to be very difficult and dangerous will vanish into thin air . . . It is intolerable that our nation should remain any longer the football for unscrupulous English politicians; at the mercy of the deliberate incitements to violence of ex-Ministers of the Crown, who are protected by their political position and their position in the English world from the justice of the law. There is the policy of trust in the Irish people and the policy of coercion. Which of these two will you have? . . . I believe that the great heart of the English people has been touched in a way it has never been touched before that for the first time you are beginning now to see the truth; to see that the claims of truth and justice require a reversal of your methods and of your Cromwellian treatment of Ireland.'

AT CHESTER

June 29th [1886]

'Coercion in Ireland has never diminished the National sentiment. It has always increased the National sentiment. It may put down political agitation for a while, I don't deny that, and you must remember that this is the meaning of coercion . . . You may stop political agitation, put down the liberty of the Press, and arrest a couple of thousand people, instead of the thousand that you did the last time – you can do all these things, but at the end of the term you were not better than you were at the beginning; and in those days of changing politics persistent recourse to coercion is impossible . . . You must be consistent in governing Ireland; and the only way you can be consistent would be to disfranchise her, deprive her of her representatives in the House of Commons, and put her outside the Constitution altogether. That is the only alternative to Mr Gladstone's method. You will have to rule Ireland as the Czar of Russia rules his subjects. So you had better look into the thing with your eyes open and see what is before you . . . If anything happened to the Liberal body at this election – I don't believe for one moment that the democracy of England will be deaf to the voice of their leaders – but if anything were to happen, if they failed in obtaining a majority at this election, it would simply mean that the whole thing would have to be done over again. After two or three years more, it would simply mean a loss of four or five years perhaps, and then you would all be invited, with the result of a great deal of bad blood and added bitterness to begin the whole work over again and to consider Mr Gladstone's plan, or somebody else's, for giving a Constitution to Ireland.'

AT A LIBERAL DEMONSTRATION AT HACKNEY, LONDON

July 4th [1886]

'No English Minister, however great, had been able to get the upper and middle classes of this country to do justice to Ireland until things had become so intolerable in that country that justice could no longer be delayed.'

'Mr Gladstone recognised the fact that reasonable regard must be had for the National sentiments of the Irish people, and in teaching that creed he had touched the hearts of the Irish nation.'

THE TORY LAND BILL

House of Commons
September 3rd [1886]

'My experience in this House has been, in reference to victories that have been carried, that nothing is got except by constant persistence. The motto, 'Try, try, try again,' is the one for the Irish members to adopt. It had been successful in the case of every movement they had made during the last eleven years, and had been for many years, from the question of the abolition of flogging in the army to the question of Irish autonomy in which I have been engaged, and which has been simply fought by constant persistence and by the exhibition of the fact that we believe in the honesty and the justice of the claims we were making.'

BANQUET TO MR JUSTIN M'CARTHY, AT THE WESTMINSTER PALACE HOTEL, LONDON

September 8th [1886]

'We can be more moderate than we were in 1879 or 1880, because our position is very much stronger. I don't say that we should be unduly moderate, but our position is a good deal different from the position of 1874 and from the position of 1879, and I believe that the Irish members and the Irish people will recognize this, that they will use those weapons of legality and of moderation which have so distinguished their cause up to the present – means which have gained for our cause the respect and sympathy of the whole civilised world – that they will follow on those lines and in this direction until they have obtained from England a settlement of the great National question. A settlement which will include all other questions; a settlement which will include the settlement of the land question and all those questions with which we are obliged to weary the English Parliament so much; a settlement which will be a lasting one and a final one, which will enable our people to go forward as a nation amongst the nations of the world in the task of regenerating our country, of developing our resources, and of attaining to that position for which, I believe, God has destined her.'

Extract from a Circular issued from the Irish Parliamentary Offices, with reference to Mr Parnell's views on the Plan of Campaign:

'Mr Parnell does not propose to express any opinion as to the 'Plan of Campaign' at present, as he is desirous of first going to

Ireland and having an opportunity of consulting with the gentlemen responsible for its organization and working, whom he has not seen since the close of last session. He also wished for further information than that at present in his possession with regard to various matters before he speaks publicly on the subject. Mr Parnell was not aware that the Plan of Campaign had been devised, or was going to be proposed, until he saw it in the newspapers.'

THE ADDRESS – MR PARNELL 'S AMENDMENT

House of Commons
February, 1887.

{During the winter of 1886, the landlords in many places had manifested a disposition to wreak vengeance upon the tenants. It was their way of celebrating the defeat of the Home Rule Bill, and the return of the Tories to power. Sir Michael Hicks-Beach, however, did his utmost to discourage this infamous scheme by delaying and obstructing evictions. The Plan of Campaign, too, taught them that their best policy was discretion.}

'My amendment also complains that the Government have been guilty of unusual, doubtful, and unconstitutional courses in Ireland during the past five months. At first sight it may be supposed that I was referring to the exercising of the dispensing power – to the pressure which the right hon. gentleman, the Chief Secretary,[25] boasted at Bristol, that he had brought upon the landlords. This is not the case. I shall have to deal with that phase of the events of last winter later on. I shall have to point out that the Government by the adoption of their Plan of Campaign – by the exercise of this pressure and of this dispensing power – have not cleared themselves from the blame which attaches to them for the rejection of the Relief Bill. I do not propose to criticise the

Government for having resorted to that method of pressure in Ireland – it was the best thing under the circumstances they could have done. It was a very poor attempt at government. The authors of the Plan of Campaign had no difficulty in outshining and in gaining far greater and more successful results than the Government could gain in the same direction . . . In your English history you will recollect that the right of public meeting was asserted by the sacrifice of many lives and the spilling of much blood at Peterloo. In Ireland we have on all occasions overwhelming forces both of military and police to contend with, and we have never been able to assert our right to public meeting in the same fashion. But I wish to know upon what authority, upon what law, by what statute, and, if by common law, under what judicial decision – for we know judicial decisions lay down the common law, and interpret the common law – did the Government in Ireland proclaim the Sligo meeting? . . . Well, sir, I also complain of the jury packing of Sligo which, I admit, is in one way about as bad as could be chosen to induce the Irish people to despise and dislike the administration of the law. What were the facts of this jury packing at the Connaught winter assizes? On a jury panel where more than one half of the jurors were Catholics, and in a province where nine-tenths of the population are Catholic, the assizes were held for the province of Connaught, three juries were struck for the trial of the agrarian cases, and not a single Catholic was allowed to put his foot into the box. A fourth jury was struck in which there was only one Roman Catholic – he was a bailiff, and under the influence of the landlord. And yet the Government expect the Irish people to believe in the justice of the administration of the law, although where three-fourths of the population of the whole country, and nine-tenths of the population of the province are Catholics, they are only allowed one single representative on the juries who tried political and agrarian offences. No wonder if, when by some chance a Catholic or two got on a jury, they make it a point of honour to occasionally disagree with the Government . . . The Plan of Campaign is, and has been, very well criticised on this part of it – that the tenants should stand together, and those that can pay should refuse to pay until those who cannot pay get a fair settlement. That is an important provision of the Plan of Campaign. Without it the tenants who cannot pay would be sacrificed. Their houses would be burned and levelled, as has happened in the case of Glenbeigh.[26] In the case of Glenbeigh, the twenty-five solvent tenants on the estate all paid – nine of them being members of the local National League, of the committee of the local National League. Where then is there evidence that the National League interfered, or that the Plan of Campaign was adopted? I say again that if these twenty-five solvent tenants had not paid, if the estate had adopted and held to the Plan of Campaign – I am not prejudicing the question of its rectitude or the reverse in what I am saying, I am simply dealing with the questions of allegation and of fact – those houses in Glenbeigh would never have been burnt, the homesteads would not have been levelled, all the civilised world would not have been shocked with this fresh example of the success of the Government of law and order in attacking the affections of the Irish people . . . I confess I was in the hopes at the end of last session that a Government which has been returned for the express purpose of showing Ireland that she should be justly governed in Westminster, that her wants would be properly and fairly attended to, would not have done all they could to prove once more to the Irish mind the truth of the bad old lesson that they must not look to this House for justice . . . But it is suggested in the Address from the Throne that the relations between landlord and tenant have been disturbed by the Plan of Campaign. Now, as one who is in no sense responsible for the bringing forward of the Plan of Campaign, I can speak freely and fairly in regard to it, and I deny in the strongest terms that there is any foundation whatever in the statement of the Address from the Throne. I believe, on the contrary, that had it not been for the Plan of Campaign, many of the tenants who have now roofs over their heads would have been sent out on the bare hillside like the Glenbeigh tenantry . . . It is evident that the Government and the authors of the Plan of Campaign aimed at precisely the same end; but the Government were not so successful . . . If in the opinion of the Law Advisers of the Government the Plan of Campaign was illegal, they should have told the Irish people that without delay, and in time – they should not have waited till estate after estate had committed themselves to this Plan, in the belief that it was perfectly constitutional, if they had determined to step in with the strong arm of what is called law in Ireland . . . The legality of the Plan is a matter which, if I had been in a position to concern myself about it, I should have desired to be satisfied of. I should have thought it necessary to take the opinion of counsel myself, and I am informed that counsel had given opinions in favour of the constitutional policy of the Plan of Campaign. However that may be, the action of the Government stands condemned, first of all in their having refrained from expressing any opinion about its legality; secondly, for having removed the case out of the Court in which it was originally taken to one in which they expected to get a subservient jury; and, thirdly, by attempting to take proceedings by a short cut before the Court of Queen's Bench, and inviting that Court to express its opinion with regard to the Plan of Campaign, which was not before the Court, and in reference to which there was no evidence whatever.'

DEBATE ON THE CLOTURE

February 21st [1887]

'A party in power always thought very little of the conservation of the liberties of debate and the protection of the minority, but a party out of power always thought a great deal of these things, and her Majesty's Government, although in a majority to-day and for a few months, ought to recollect that for fifty years, even under the old restricted franchise, they (the Conservatives) were more often in a minority than in a majority, and in all probability that state of affairs would be intensified in fifty years to come, and it would be they who would have to regret, and not the Irish members, that they had done something – feeble it was true, but still as much as they were able – to injure the rights of minorities in the country . . . The present rules would not be effectual in forwarding public business, they would only prove effectual in limiting the rights of minorities, and, to some extent, throttling debate. Members of minorities made valuable suggestions from time to time. He considered, as one who had been in a minority ever since he had been in the House, now eleven years, and as one who felt he would always be in a minority as long as he was in that House, that he might be allowed to plume himself on making valuable suggestions which had since been embodied in statute form. He could never have made those suggestions had the rules been altered as the Government now proposed . . . If the Government would boldly grapple with this question, and would pay some regard to the diversified interests and varied nationalities of which this Empire was composed; if they would, instead of adopting penal and restrictive measures – measures directed against the life, the utility, and well-being of minorities – remodelled their machinery, or constructed fresh machines of such a character as would be likely to prove effectual, they would be richly rewarded, and they would find that the dignity of the House, so far from being lessened would be increased.'

MR PARNELL'S AMENDMENT EXEMPTING COERCION ACTS
FROM THE OPERATION OF THE RULES

February 24th [1887]

'The House will see that the rule is a very startling and a very
alarming innovation. Under the old system it was necessary that
the evident sense of the House should be manifested in support of
the cloture, and that the Speaker should be of opinion that the
question had been adequately discussed. There is nothing in the
rule as to the evident sense of the House, and nothing as to an
adequate discussion of the question. What are the contingencies
that we will have to look forward to in view of the application of
this very stringent and alarmingly altered rule under the circumstances that I have suggested? We may have to look forward to a
time of public excitement in this country when the Ministers may
think it their absolute duty in proposing a Coercion Act – as they
always thought it their absolute duty – to pass it with rapidity.
Before our time it used to be the custom to pass Coercion Acts
through the Houses of Parliament in a single day by the suspension
of the standing orders. That has not been the case since 1875 . . .
The right hon. gentleman, the leader of the House (Mr W. H. Smith)
says it is not his intention to use this rule in an arbitrary way or to
stop debate unfairly, but the road to a certain place is paved with
good intentions, and we know very well what becomes of the good
intentions of a Minister when a time of turbulence and difficulty
and danger arises, when Ministers lose their heads, and when
members of Parliament get carried away by the excitement of the
moment. We should be false to all our duties and regardless of our
trust it we did not most strongly protest against the possibility of
such a contingency as that which I have suggested. When Coercion
Bills are proposed Ministers are always exceedingly anxious to get
them passed through very quickly. I have never known an occasion
when the Ministers in charge of a Coercion Bill did not think it

absolutely necessary that the Act should be given to them without a moment's delay; but, under the Constitution as it now exists, with 85 members coming from Ireland pledged to oppose coercion, with 200 English Liberal members here on these benches pledged also to oppose coercion for Ireland, and with many Conservative members, followers of her Majesty's Government, pledged also to oppose coercion for Ireland, I ask is it not right that we should test the opinion of this House with regard to the matter? Is it not right that while we have time we should seek to insert some safeguards in this rule which will prevent the Ministers who have charge of the Bill from acting in an arbitrary fashion and preventing freedom of speech, which is so necessary in the discussion of a Coercion Act.'

DEBATE ON THE CLOTURE

March 1st [1887]

'He looked upon the position of the Irish members in the House as one necessitating above all things that they should strive for such protections as that which he was asking the House to adopt, because even the so-called Unionists, who had announced that it was their intention to have one Parliament, and to have Irishmen fully represented in that Parliament, had shown that they looked upon the Irish members as being not so good as themselves, and as being unworthy of having the same measure meted out to them as would be meted out to an English party in opposition. He had seen, in their British good opinion of themselves, that they considered that the fair play and the justice and the toleration which they extended to their British political opponents were thought too good for their Irish political opponents . . . Those feelings of consideration, of fair play, and of toleration which had always marked the putting of rules of this kind in force by one of the two English political parties against the other was absent when either party was contending with its Irish opponents.'

DEBATE ON THE CONSTABULARY VOTE

March 3rd [1887]

'The hon. gentleman (the Chief Secretary for Ireland[27]) said distinctly that the next time those who attended suppressed meetings should expect something harder than batons. What did "harder than batons" mean? The police carried something harder than batons – they carried cold steel, and with that the hon. gentleman had threatened the future litigants, the people who were aggrieved persons. What was the authority upon which the Chief Secretary was entitled to order his policemen to meetings to disperse them by force of arms, and to give the people attending these meetings and refusing to disperse cold steel, as something harder than batons? What was the authority for that? Were they to wait in vain for an answer? . . . What was the law upon which they relied, and where was their authority?'

DEBATE ON THE ARREST OF FATHER KELLER, P. P., OF YOUGHAL[28]

March 18th [1887]

'Your "strong and stern" Government is due to the exigencies of your party, and not to the exigencies of the state of affairs in Ireland. A year ago your party deliberately turned their back upon the stern enforcement of the law because it suited your purpose as a party. To-day it suits your purpose as a party to imprison priests and to uphold what you call the law with the sternness and resoluteness of the right hon. gentleman the Chief Secretary. Well, with neither of these feelings can I sympathise – upon neither of these attempts at government can I look with anything but the contempt that they deserve.'

DEBATE ON THE COERCION BILL

April 1st [1887]

'It was not until last night that this House and the country were put in possession of the general and complete policy of the Government in its nakedness and dishonesty. The proceedings last night, sir, in another place (the Cabinet Council) revealed to us the extent of the plot and the gravity of the conspiracy by which it is intended by the Tory party and the Liberal Unionists on the one side to coerce, if possible, the tenants of Ireland into the payment of impossible rents, and on the other side to compel the purchase of the landlord's interest at exorbitant prices, at prices which will most certainly lead to repudiation on a wholesale scale and to a great loss to the British taxpayer. Up to the present we have only had the coercion side, the direct coercion side, of the Government; but last night in another place we were treated to what I may call the indirect coercion side of the Government – a species of coercion which, under the pretext of conferring benefits on the Irish people, stabs them in the back – a species of coercion which, under the guise of friendship, inflicts a most deadly injury . . .What do you propose to do now as part of your remedial legislation? You propose to give to twenty-five county court judges the duty of deciding whether 450,000 Irish tenants are in the first instance persons of good character; whether, in the second place, their inability to pay rent is due to the fact that they have taken too much whiskey, or that the land is too poor; and, in the third place, what the fair rent is to be that they ought to pay in the future. A more monstrous proposal never entered the brain of man . . . It is a proposal that is bound to break down from the very commence-ment . . . It is the old story. In proportion to the severity of your coercion code the efficiency of your remedial measures will be diminished. In proportion as you strike down Irish liberties so will be the ratio of the lessened efficiency of the ameliorating courts, such as the courts of the Land Commission and others you may establish in Ireland for the redress of Irish grievances . . . I am convinced that if the landlord party in the House of Commons had not previously got the Coercion Act of 1881 passed they would have allowed a far better and more generous Land Act to have passed through both this House and the House of Lords, and that Act would not have been foredoomed to failure by reason of its own inefficiency from the very moment of its birth. If you handicap the Irish tenants in their struggle against unjust rents, if you throw the power into the landlords' hands in Ireland, depend upon it your imperfect attempts to do justice to the tenants will be foredoomed to failure, and that it will be impossible for them to contend against the obstacles which will be placed in their way . . . If you attempt to float the landlords by means of State credit the result must surely be wholesale repudiation on the part of those who are forced to purchase . . . From first to last I have never wavered or faltered for a single moment in the belief that in the direction of land purchase lies your hope of settling the Irish question . . . That has been our position – to make the Irish tenant the owner of his holding, and we believe he will turn the sands into gold. We believe if this be done on a fair basis and a fair price in the absence of coercion, not with coercion, that the Irish tenant will fulfil his obligations to the last penny, and the result will be satisfactory to the English nation and without risk to the British Exchequer.'

THE DEBATE ON THE ADDRESS

February 13th [1888]

'It would appear from all we have heard that England is, but Ireland is not, to be given a Local Government, because it would be used as an engine to resist the Coercion Act. It marks the great advance which has been made by the Conservative party in the downward course of coercion, that whereas they came into office stating their determination to carry Local Government for the Irish counties *pari passu*, or almost so with Local Government for the English counties, we now find after little more than a year of Conservative rule in Ireland the condition of the country has become so bad that it is impossible to entrust the Irish counties with the right of levying rates for building bridges and repairing roads. . . It is now twelve years since I entered public life, and at a time when very few believed in Parliamentary agitation. For one who favoured Parliamentary agitation, there were ten who looked to violence and revolution as the true means of saving Ireland. But all that is changed now. I think you may reverse those figures now. That is great progress to have made. I believe that progress will not be undone – that the hands of the clock will not be set back by the puny attempts of the right hon. gentleman. The Irish people will continue to laugh at his coercion, and to look to the future with hope and the assured knowledge that their country is on the eve of prosperity and progress. I should wish the right hon. gentleman were more sensible of the gravity and tension of the situation. The Irish tenant will pay his rent as long as he has the money to pay. Is that denied? Who denies it? You are dumb! All the king's horses and all the king's men won't be able to get the people to pay when they have not got the money. That is the agrarian situation in Ireland. You say the agrarian question is the whole Irish question. Why, in the name of common sense, don't you settle it? . . . There is one thing I must draw attention to before I sit down, and it is the treatment of the political prisoners – because, if they are not political prisoners they are nothing. It is useless for the Government to say these men are criminals. That plea has been urged by every tyrant in excuse for torturing his political opponents, and it will not avail the right hon. gentleman now any more than it availed any of his predecessors, or any of those infamous characters in ancient history, who did not draw the line between political and other prisoners.'

MR PARNELL'S ARREARS BILL

March 21st [1888]

'This is a pressing question, and it needs immediate action. The greatest trouble in connexion with all your attempts to deal with this land question has been that you have been too late – sometimes two years too late, sometimes one year too late. In '86 I asked the House to abate the judicial rents. It refused, and a year later it abated them. But you were too late. In the meantime this load of arrears had accumulated – arrears of rent which by that act of abatement you admitted to be excessive. The land question is a very good illustration for us, and such action – if hostile action is taken against this bill today – is the best argument we could have in England, in Ireland, everywhere in favour of the restoration of a Parliament for Ireland. It is an excellent illustration of the impossibility of governing Ireland from Westminster by the votes of English members under the direction of English public opinion. Your muddling and messing with this question is the best illustration we could have . . . How is it you cannot settle the Irish land question? In the first place you know nothing at all about it. You go to Birmingham instead of to Ireland for your guides[29]. . . It will never be possible for you, no matter how much you try, to settle the Irish land question, to govern Ireland with the consent of the people. You will always have her people arrayed in hostility against any attempt to deprive her in perpetuity of those rights which were given her in 1782; and, I believe, if the Irish land question was settled to-morrow upon the most absolutely fair basis, that it would in no respect diminish the strength of our claim for the restitution of our Irish Parliament.'

DEBATE ON THE ENNIS OUTRAGE

Thursday, April 12th [1888]

{On April 8th a public meeting was set upon by a strong force of police and cavalry. The people were batoned and sabred in the most cruel manner, though utterly unable to offer any resistance.}

'Sir, when I read on last Monday of what had happened at Ennis, my blood boiled at the horrible result of the barbarity there perpetrated, and it was with difficulty I could restrain myself from taking immediate notice of the attacks on the people; but I saw it was the right of the Chief Secretary to have ample opportunity of giving any excuses he could, and of presenting this horrible occurrence in some different light than that which it has been presented to the public by no less than three different newspapers . . . The right hon. gentleman has said there was stone-throwing – I think he said showers of stones. He said to-day some stones were thrown from the building in question before the attack was made by the police on the people, before the baton charge was ordered. He also stated that to the best of his information he does not believe stones were thrown from the yard in question; and I will confine myself to the incidents that took place in the yard – to what was done by the people in the yard, and what was done to the people in the yard by the police and soldiers. I shall ask the House to agree with me that because stones were thrown at the police from the top of the building there was no reason why the people who were in the yard should be attacked and assaulted in the way they were . . . We have the statement of the right hon. the Chief Secretary that some stones were thrown from the top of this store. We have it advanced as the only excuse and defence for the attack of the police. I submit it is not an excuse for the attack by the police. It is not an excuse for permitting Colonel Turner[30] to order the constables to rush pell-mell into the yard – into an enclosed yard – and to baton unfortunate people indiscriminately. It is not an excuse for Colonel Turner to order the hussars, with drawn sabres, into this enclosed yard, to slash right and left; and it was no excuse for ordering the foot soldiers into the yard with fixed bayonets, when the people were quiet and using no force . . . If you persist in this course, all I say is that, the responsibility upon the heads of the Irish Executive and upon the head of the Chief Secretary will be a very grave one if there should be loss of life. By all means put your Coercion Act in force as you have got it. You have seen that imprisonment has no terror for the Irish people. But that is no reason why you should invent new punishments – these infamous attacks and assaults by the armed forces of the Crown . . . If the right hon. gentleman wishes to proclaim Martial Law let him do so, and then the people would know what they had to expect. But let him not take the matter into his own hands.'

THE LAND COMMISSION BILL

April 30th [1888]

'Turning to the question of appeal, Mr Parnell expressed his belief that it would have been better had there been no appeal from the decisions of Sub-Commissioners, because appeals had proved a drag to the working of the Land Act of 1881, which had almost overwhelmed it, and in many cases rendered it nugatory. If by this Bill they offered further inducements to the landlords to swamp the courts with appeals, they would simply stop the working of the Land Act of 1881 and 1885.'

At a Banquet given by Mr Parnell to the members of the Irish Party, in honour of those colleagues who have suffered under the Coercion Act, in proposing the toast of 'Our Guests,' he said:

'I am happy to say, gentlemen, that upon this occasion, as on every other occasion, the spirit and the courage of Irishmen did not fail them, and that there have not been found wanting men, women, and children wherever called upon throughout the length and breadth of Ireland to face this imprisonment, cruel and harsh as it is, disgraceful as it has been sought to be made, without flinching, and happy that it is their lot to suffer for their country. Amongst these have been foremost our guests. We are proud that from amongst the Irish Parliamentary Party men have been chosen to undergo this suffering. We are proud that they have not flinched from their duty, and that they have shown from the highest to the lowest that they know how to follow in the footsteps of those who have encountered greater dangers, even death itself, for Ireland. And while we honour our guests we also honour the humbler men – the obscurer men and women who, without any position to uphold, have seen their duty and have done it; who, because they are obscure men, are selected by the tyrant who now presumes to direct the affairs of Ireland – have been selected for keener and more bitter punishment, for you well know that Mr Balfour had made a degradation these men's imprisonment. These victims were not much before the public gaze – these obscurer persons, the news-vendors, the humble shopkeepers throughout the country, who, as officers of the National League branches have to do their duty, and have done their duty just as courageously as our guests who have upheld the right of freedom of speech and of combination through-out the length and breadth of the country. These obscure people have been selected by Mr Balfour for excessive punishment, which even he would not dare to inflict upon a member of Parliament.'

DEBATE ON THE ADDRESS

House of Commons
March 1st, 1889

{On the evening of this day London was startled by the intelligence that Richard Pigott, the author of the forged letters published by the *Times*, had been arrested in Madrid, whither he had fled on the exposure of his crime, and that the unhappy wretch had, in his despair, committed suicide. Mr Parnell appeared in his place in the House of Commons, a few hours later, and his entrance was marked by a scene of enthusiasm such as had never, perhaps, been witnessed in Parliament. He was the one member in the crowded House who seemed to be absolutely unmoved by the extraordinary demonstration, and, his speech contained no reference to his own vindication and triumph. His thoughts were with the political prisoners.}

'I desire, sir, to express some words of sympathy with my colleagues who have suffered and are suffering in Ireland by the unscrupulous means adopted by the right honorable gentleman (Mr Balfour). I sympathize with my friends who have bravely counter-worked the present Government in Ireland, and I believe that they will be richly rewarded in the near future by the victory which patient suffering always in the end wins . . . It is useless for the Government to plead, as they have pleaded, that they are but administering the law, and that the law does not permit them to alter the system of prison treatment. The law is as they made it. I do not wish to remind the House of the means by which they obtained the urgency, and of the conspiracy which assisted them on the very night of the second reading, to steal away the liberties of Ireland. They will have either to stand or fall by this law as it now stands.

{After referring to the prison treatment of the Irish members, he continued}

... We think less of them and of their sufferings than we do of the humblest men in our ranks. And why? Because these humble men have not the same chance in their fight against your system. You cannot kill Mr O'Brien.[31] You dare not kill him. You cannot torture Mr Carew[32] to death. But how about the others? How about the less known men who are not members of Parliament – men like John Mandeville[33] – who were done to death in carrying out this policy, men who were done to death in carrying out this system, and neces[s]arily done to death if you must carry out this system? How about Larkin, who was convicted of the same political offences as those committed by Mr O'Brien and Mr Carew? It is for those men we have the most sympathy, because the fight for them is not an equal one.'

AT THE 'EIGHTY CLUB'

March 8th [1889]

'There is only one way by which you can govern Ireland within the constitution, and that is by allowing her to govern herself in all these matters which cannot interfere with the greatness and the well-being of the empire of which she forms a part. I admit there is another, and that is a way which has not been tried yet. It is a way that probably never will be tried . . . There is a way in which you might obtain, at all events, some present success in the government of Ireland; it is not Mr Balfour's bastard-plan of a semi-constitution and a semi-coercive method. It would be a method of pure despotism. You might find amongst yourselves some great Englishman or Scotchman who would go over to Ireland, her Parliamentary representation having been taken away from her, and who would do justice to her people notwithstanding the complaints of Irish landlordism. Such a man might be found, who, on the one hand would oppose a stern front to the inciters to revolution or outrage, and on the other hand would check the exorbitant demand of the landlords and officials in the country, and perhaps the result might be successful, but it would have to be a method outside the constitution. Both on the one side and on the other your Irish governor would have full power to check the evil doer whether the evil doer was a lord or a peasant, whether the malefactor hailed from Westminster or New York. The power would be equally exercised and constantly maintained. In that way, perhaps, you might govern Ireland for a season. That, in my judgment from the first time I entered political life, appeared to me to be the only alternative of the concession to Ireland of full power over her own domestic interest and her future. In one way only, I also saw, could the power and influence of a constitutional party be banded together within the limits of the law; by acting on those principles laid down by Lucas and Gavan Duffy in 1852, that they should hold themselves aloof from all English political parties and combinations, that they should refuse place and office for themselves or for their friends or their relations, and that the Irish constituencies should refuse to return any member who was a traitor to those pledges.'

MEETING AT ST JAMES'S HALL, LONDON,
TO PROTEST AGAINST COERCION

March 13th [1889]

'Meetings like this show to my countrymen everywhere that for the first time in 1886 they were admitted by the English people into terms of equal union and good fellowship with them. I prefer to draw lessons from passing events, and I think we all prefer to draw these lessons to press them home, rather than to claim any party or passing triumph. What, then, has been one of the results of that system (the system of misgovernment and coercion)? That we the Irish members from the very necessity of our position are unable to take that share in the duties of government which is one of the hopes and justifiable hopes of all men who become members of Parliament. And if we did, if we violated the pledges on which alone we have obtained the trust of our constituencies – namely, that we should refuse to accept place or office for ourselves or for others from any English Government so long as the just rights of Ireland were not conceded; if any one of us were so base or so mean as to break that pledge and to accept office, the result would be that throughout the length and breadth of Ireland we should fail to find a single constituency which would re-elect us . . . The land of Ireland has had, so far as it has had any added value conferred upon it by labour and artificial means, all that value was conferred upon it by the occupying tenants and their predecessors in title . . . The owners have mainly lived out of the country, and they have avoided, so far as they possibly could, any expenditure whatever upon the holdings of their tenants, and so it happens that the lands have been fenced, drained and reclaimed, so far as those works were effected, by the labour of the tenants. The houses have been built by the tenants, and you Englishmen and Englishwomen ought to reflect when you read of the forcible resistance made in some cases by Irish tenants against the armed constabulary and emergency-men – is a resistance which is not real resistance, because it amounts to such resistance as a fly might make to an elephant who was about to put its foot upon it – but when you hear of these instances you must reflect that after all these men and women are being turned out of their holdings and out of their homes which they have built for themselves, and which are their own property, although the law has not yet efficiently protected that property, but which are their own property just as much as the mill of the Lancashire mill-owner is his property.'

PRESENTATION OF ADDRESSES FROM THE
MUNICIPAL BODIES OF IRELAND TO MR PARNELL AT THE
WESTMINSTER PALACE HOTEL, LONDON, CONGRATULATING
HIM ON THE COLLAPSE OF THE PIGOTT CONSPIRACY

{It is to be observed that Mr Parnell disdained to make any allusion to the *Times*' plot and to his own sufferings when addressing English audiences. Speaking to his countrymen his proud reserve gave way.}

[May 23rd, 1889]

'I should have preferred to have gone to my grave with the stigma of these letters upon me – cowardly, mean, and contemptible as these letters were – rather than submit my country and my countrymen to the humiliating ordeal that was forced upon us as the accompaniment of the inquiry into the authenticity of these letters . . . We did not accept this Commission. We do not – we never have acknowledged the justice of the reference. We did not admit, we never have admitted, by any word or act of ours that this tribunal was a fair tribunal, or one of a character and constitution competent to inquire into the issues laid before it. For these issues, as they have been put before the commission of judges, are not issues which can ever be decided by any earthly tribunal . . . I believe the verdict of history will be on our side; but there are questions which, from their very nature, must be left to history to settle, and no tribunal of judges, ignorant of the history of Ireland, knowing nothing of the character of her people without information as to the surrounding circumstances – by education, birth, feeling and habits of thought, political conviction, and training averse to the aspirations of Ireland – no such tribunal is fitted or able to decide the grave issues that have been laid before this Commission for decision. . . I believe that our cause is so good and so strong, and that our position to-day stands so clear before the public opinion of the world, that even under all these disadvantages which I have recited to you, even with the dice loaded against us, and with the cards – with the trump card, as they had hoped – up their sleeves, we shall come out of this far-reaching inquiry untouched and unharmed, but brightened by the trial, and that our country will stand clearer and prouder than when she entered upon this ordeal. . . If our constitutional movement were to fail I would not continue twenty-four hours at Westminster. The most advanced section of Irishmen, as well as the least advanced, have always thoroughly understood that the Parliamentary policy was to be a trial, and that we did not ourselves believe in any possibility of maintaining for all time or for any lengthened period an incorrupt and independent Irish representation at Westminster.'

DEBATE ON THE GOVERNMENT LAND PURCHASE BILL

House of Commons
April 21st, 1890

'We do not fear the solution of the land question. We know that as you give independence and security to the Irish tenant, so his worth as an Irishman and as an Irish nationalist will be increased. We do not base our claim upon nationhood or the sufferings and calamities of our countrymen. We use these rather as illustrations of your incapacity to govern us, and to do justice from Westminster. But these things are not the foundation of Ireland's claim to her restitution of legislative independence. So far from the securing of the tenant in his holding, or the solution of the land question pre-venting a settlement of the great National question, I am convinced that every injustice that is removed, every tenant who is secured in the future, increases the force of the great army which is arrayed on our side for the liberation of our country.'

MOTION FOR THE ADJOURNMENT
POLICE OUTRAGES AT TIPPERARY AND CASHEL

June 9th [1890]

'The Chief Secretary is armed with very important and extensive powers. He has practically, through his agents in Ireland, the power of life and death, and I think that the country and the House ought to insist that these powers are used not unnecessarily, and with judgment and discretion. If there is to be action of a punitive character, it should be taken from the point of view of the right hon. gentleman, not against poor people like the ignorant peasants, who have suffered on this occasion, but against those whom the right hon. gentleman could consider to be ringleaders and responsible persons . . . The people of Tipperary have gone on into this struggle. They may be right or they may be wrong. That question is not concerned here; but whether they are right or whether they are wrong, they have gone into it out of a feeling of loyalty to their leaders and to their country; and it is because they think honestly that they are doing their duty to their country in the only way possible for them to do it, that a better fate and a better treatment should have been extended to them than the horrible and infamous brutality related to us to-night by my hon. friend the Member for East Mayo.[34] If there is law on the side of the right hon. gentleman, why does he not show it by taking proceedings against my hon. friends? and why does he select the poorer and more obscure persons for his ill-treatment? It has been said that all these peasants have open access to the Courts . . . We know these things, and it is a mockery – it is worse then a mockery – to tell the Tipperary peasant, after his brains have been dashed out by the police, to take an action at law for the purpose of receiving damages . . . If you wish to have the law upheld in Ireland, let the poor people see it is made for them as much as it is for their betters.'

Part III

Betrayed!

✦

'May the brand of shame on the Irish brow
For ever and ever burn,
And the banded nations from their midst
A nation's outcasts spurn'

FANNY PARNELL

MANIFESTO TO THE IRISH PEOPLE

November 28th [1890]

{The secret history of the Great Betrayal has yet to he written, but no information need be expected just yet from those who could perhaps explain away the mystery of the sudden change by which the devoted Parnellites of the Leinster Hall meeting became the servile Whigs of Committee Room No. 15. The public events which preceded, attended and followed the historic revolt of the Seceders are, however, fresh in the public mind, and need not be narrated here. In any case, it should suffice for Irishmen to know that a majority of their representatives sacrificed as a peace-offering to British hypocrisy and cant, the greatest Irishman of this age, and that a majority of Irishmen at home were base enough to applaud the deed of national disgrace.}

'I believe that party (the Irish party) will obtain Home Rule only provided it remains independent of any English party.'

Facsimile of Portion of Mr Parnell's Famous
Manifesto to the Irish People. Dated Nov 28th 1890

(?)

your intervention would soon have been necessary
to save many of your Parliamentary representatives from
falling under the domination of English Parties,
and to remind them that Ireland considers
the independency of her members as her only
safe-guard within the Constitution, and above
and beyond all other considerations whatever.

The threat in that letter repeated so insolently
on many English platforms and in numerous
British newspapers that unless
Ireland concedes this right of veto to England,
she will indefinitely postpone her chances of
obtaining legislative Home Rule independence, compels
me, while not for one moment admitting
the slightest probability of such loss, to
put before you information which until
now has been solely in my possession
and which will enable you to
understand what it is that you are threatened with
the loss of — unless you consent to throw us to the English
wolves now howling for my destruction.

MR PARNELL'S SPEECH IN COMMITTEE ROOM NO. 15

'The men whose ability is now so conspicuously exercised as that of Mr Healy and Mr Sexton, will have to bear their responsibility for this . . . Why did you encourage me to come forward and maintain my leadership in the face of the world if you were not going to stand by me? . . . I want to ask you before you vote my deposition to be sure you are getting value for it . . . I know what Mr Gladstone will do for you; I know what Mr Morley will do for you; and I know there is not a single one of the lot to be trusted unless you trust yourselves. Be to your own selves true and hence it follows, as the day the night, thou can'st not be false to any man . . . If I am to leave you to-night I should like to leave you in security. I should like, and it is not an unfair thing for me to ask, that I should come within sight of the Promised Land; that I should come with you, having come so far, if not to the end of this course, that I should at least come with you as far as you will allow and permit me to come with you, at least until it is absolutely sure that Ireland and I can go no further.'

TO REPRESENTATIVE OF 'EVENING TELEGRAPH' AFTER THE BETRAYAL

'Tell them I will fight to the end.'

ADDRESSING A CROWD IN THE EARLY MORNING OF DECEMBER 10TH FROM DR KENNY'S HOUSE, DUBLIN

[1890]

'And with the youth of Ireland I feel confident we shall win, and that the common sense and judgment of our people will rally in the true path, and will refuse to allow our country to be guided by the dictation of any man however eminent.'

IN REPLY TO ADDRESS FROM DUBLIN LEADERSHIP

Same date [December 10th 1890]

'For the sake of the future of the country I am here to lead you not astray. I have never led you astray yet. I shall not today lie false to your traditions or mine, but I shall insist that Ireland shall decide this question for herself.'

PUBLIC MEETING AT ROTUNDA

December 10th [1890]

'I tell you, fellow-countrymen, that when the day comes for measuring the amount of my shortcomings, and the amount of my opponents' shortcomings, the balance will not be against me . . . God knows it was not a time when I was crippled in strength, when it was doubtful whether I might ever again come before you. God knows that it was not a time to confront me with a movement of mutiny stronger, more vindictive, more disgraceful, and more cowardly than any commander-in-chief has ever been called upon to face. They bided their time, and they thought that I was dead, and that they might play round my corpse, and divert the Irish nation from the true issues involved. They reckoned without taking an account of the undying resolution of our race . . . We shall know some day who has done this deadly thing against Ireland? . . . If you have any fault to find with me now is the time to bring it forward. I don't pretend to be immaculate. I don't pretend that I had not had moments of trial and of temptation; but I do claim that never in thought, in word, or deed have I been false to the trust that Irishmen have confided in me . . . To what else could I look but the young men of Ireland.'

INTERVIEW WITH 'NEW YORK WORLD' REPRESENTATIVE

December [1890]

'Mr Gladstone's obstinacy on the one hand, and the ignorance and inexperience of so many members of the party on the other, produced the catastrophe . . . There is no doubt that the Liberal party is bound to Home Rule, and cannot come into power without it. In proportion as the independence and integrity of the party is lost, so a measure of Home Rule is diminished, and the stronger and more independent we remain, the larger, better, and more satisfactory will be the settlement.'

AT KILKENNY DURING ELECTION CONTEST

December 12th [1890]

'Having spent sixteen years in the service of my country, I think I ought to know how she can best be led to victory.'

AT GORESBRIDGE

December 18th [1890]

'I tell you, men of Kilkenny and of Carlow, that I will submit to no English dictation; that I hold my position as leader of the Irish people, upon no English sufferance, and that I look to the people of Ireland for my orders and for my instructions, and to no other . . . You know I will never sell you . . . I will go on and prosper, with Ireland helping me I fear no enemy.'

AT KILKENNY

December 20th [1890]

'I respect the motives of everybody, even the motives of the men who threw lime into my eyes at Castlecomer – and I know the day will come, and come very soon, when these men will be the first to acknowledge how misguided was their action . . . While I have my life, I will go from one constituency to another, from one city to another, from one town and village and parish to another to put what I know is the truth before the people . . . To the voice of Ireland alone I will bow. I will not yield to English dictation.'

{In answer to an attack of Mr Davitt, during Kilkenny contest.}

'I am what I am, because I am known to be an honest and unchanging Irishman.'

AT KILKENNY

December 21st [1890]

'The men who were elected in 1885 to fill the Irish seats were men who were elected for a particular work; but they were not elected to sit in judgment on me . . . And I shall regard myself still as your commanding officer, carrying the banner, wielding your strong and sharp swords, clearing our way through every opposition, through every foe, *to the death if necessary*, to the bitter end . . . If I have faithfully defended your cause with all the energy and all the strength that my weak frame is capable of, then I say, fellow-countrymen *you ought to* allow me to accompany you a little further on this bright path which, I verily believe, is before us . . . You ought not strike me back from you just as we are at the gate of victory.'

AT KILKENNY AFTER THE DEFEAT

'We shall again form a self-respecting and a strong party, and, being once more strong, shall claim as we claimed before, the respect of the two English parties.'

AT KILDARE EN ROUTE FOR DUBLIN

'I claim for Ireland, as I have always claimed for her, the right of deciding her own destinies, of electing her own members, and of electing her own leaders. Surrender your free choice of your own members and your leader to no Englishman however illustrious, and keep your members as long as you have members at Westminster, keep them free from contamination from English parties, from English politicians, and from English clubs. Guard them, and if they are weak, for there is always danger of weakness; and I have never concealed it from you, that there has been danger to your cause and to your representation in the powerful engines of contamination which these English parties have ready at hand . . . But you, fellow-countrymen, will show, when the time comes, that you will not be corrupted to one side; that you will keep your head straight to the enemy; and that you will make your members keep their heads straight to the enemy.'

AT NATIONAL CLUB, DUBLIN, AFTER KILKENNY DEFEAT

'I am blamed for refusing to leave Ireland – I won't say to the mercy of Mr Gladstone, but I will say to the rag-tag and bob-tail of the English Liberal party, and of the English Press. These men did not give me my commission, and I will not receive my dismissal from them . . . I am blamed again for refusing to leave Ireland and her future to the care of the forty-four gentlemen who seceded from me in No. 15 Committee Room. Now let us examine for a moment into the composition of these forty-four leaders, the future guardians of Ireland. There are sixteen of them very able and respectable persons; these sixteen are very able, and know how to take care of themselves. I don't know if their capacity will extend to the care of their fellow-countrymen. They are sixteen lawyers, solicitors and barristers . . . These sixteen gentlemen are the salt and aristocracy of this great movement of secession . . . The bar of Ireland was at one time a patriotic body, but it unhappily ceased to be a patriotic body when we lost our Parliament, and it will never again be a patriotic body until a self-governed Irish nation shows these legal gentlemen that the only way of preferment is through the hearts of their fellow-countrymen . . . I have lost no friends, no soldiers, no officers upon whom I have really depended for the direction of the National cause.'

AT THURLES

January 11th, 1891.

'There are times, fellow-countrymen, when the wheat is separated from the chaff, and when parties are weighed, not by their numbers, but by their quality and determination . . . Those who left the path will return to it, or be banished from the power to do mischief in Ireland.'

AT LIMERICK

January 12th [1891]

'We entered into an honourable alliance – an alliance, if you will, of a weaker nation, but still of a nation with a nation – and for you I claim, for the Irish people I claim, that the decision on all matters relating to your own affairs, and to your interest and business, shall be decided by you and you alone . . . I have not sought to stir up strife, and I will not seek to stir it up. I know what strife is, and God knows we don't want to enter into any battle unnecessarily, but if they drive us into a battle we will fight it out.'

AT TRALEE

January 18th [1891]

'We are told we must have regard to English public opinion – to the opinion of English statesmen. I am perfectly willing to regard English public opinion where it is just and well-informed, and where it has reference to subjects of English interest or Imperial interest and concern; but where the question is a question which only concerns Ireland, then, I say, I will not regard English public opinion. Another great difficulty is not English public opinion, but it is Irish Protestant opinion; and, fellow-countrymen, it is of the utmost importance that we should do everything we reasonably can to assuage the alarms of those men who live amongst us in every quarter of Ireland, in greater or lesser numbers, to give them every guarantee that is possible that they will not be injured in property or sentiment when Ireland recovers the right to rule herself – and not only to give this assurance and guarantee, but to abstain from any action tending to show that any section of the Irish electors allow any religious body to influence their opinions. I know of no greater mischief from this point of view than could be done to the Irish National cause than the action of certain persons during the Kilkenny election, which unhappily has been followed up in many parts of Ireland by an activity and a course of conduct from the same body of a most deplorable character. I for one raise my voice against this, and I appeal to the manhood of Ireland to say that they are sufficiently intelligent and sufficiently independent to make up their minds upon the great issue before the public without the exercise of any undue influence . . . I shall keep a firm grip until I know that you are going to get the kind of Home Rule that you expect to get, and I am young enough to fight this question on until we succeed in winning it together.'

AT CELBRIDGE

January 25th [1891]

'Ireland will have nothing to regret, nothing to blame herself for, because she has shown her independence and superiority over English intrigue and dictation.'

AT WATERFORD

January 28th [1891]

{Waterford has since splendidly vindicated Mr Parnell's judgment.}

'The manly attitude that you have taken up on this question has instructed the English people on the Irish question in a way that they were never taught before . . . The Liberal party have a much greater interest in the settlement of this question even than you have; they must settle it, or they cannot return to power . . . You will get a Parliament of some kind or another, but the sort of Parliament that you get depends entirely on yourselves. One should not be generous at the expense of a nation or a nation's aspirations . . . The Liberal Party and Mr Gladstone know what Ireland wants. There can be no mistake about it that we want a Parliament with full power to manage the affairs of Ireland, without trenching on any Imperial prerogative, or injuring any Imperial or English interest, but a Parliament we must have that will be supreme with regard to Irish questions. We will have no English veto. An English veto, whether on the appointment of your leader, or on the laws that you shall make, would break down and destroy that Parliament before it had been two years in existence. I hope that in the days and years to come the standpoint from which I have approached it will appear creditable to myself. If I had believed that you could have lost anything by standing by me,

I would never have allowed this issue to go before you . . . Ireland and England will ultimately say that the Leader of Ireland was right. . .The heart of Ireland is sound, and you must not reckon in the ranks of the opponents of Ireland every man who makes a fool of himself to-day, because the prescience and the knowledge of public affairs, and the patriotism which you have in your hearts is not given to every Irishman. We should keep our tempers at the same time we will keep our grip, and we will show an example, as statesmen of knowledge and prescience to the rest of Ireland.'

AT ATHENRY

January 31st [1891]

'I think there is no more beautiful prayer in the language than that which we sometimes address to the Almighty to have mercy on all slaves and captives! and, surely, if it was only that they were prisoners and captives the Irish people would be touched with sympathy for the men who have spent long years in penal servitude, and they would desire that the prison gates would be open and the captives set free . . . You will see that the public opinion of the world will respect you for what you have done. They would have scorned you if you had done otherwise. They would have considered you cowardly and unworthy the position of freemen if you had taken either your politics or your morality, or even your religion, from any English teacher.'

AT ENNIS

February 1st [1891]

'You have shown every enemy of Irish National rights, every pretended friend of her cause, every coward and traitor in our ranks, that Ireland will submit to no force, that she will refuse to be guided by any traitor or treason-monger, and that knowing the strength of her own position, and, above all, knowing what she wants, and being determined to obtain it, she will fight this battle out as long as an Irishman remains on Irish soil to fight it.'

AT STROKESTOWN

February 22nd [1891]

'I should have gladly and cheerfully adhered to my part of the bargain, but the touchstone which I applied to the sincerity of the Liberal faith proved that that sincerity was tinsel, and that if Ireland attempted to rely upon the professions of friendship of Radical Members of the House of Commons she would find, sooner or later, that she leaned upon a broken reed, which would pierce her hand, and ruin and destroy the future interests of our nation.'

AT LONGFORD

February 22nd [1891]

'I took off my coat for the purpose of obtaining and consummating the future of Irish nationality. That position was accepted by the men of Ireland, and upon that position I have stood during these long years . . . I shall stand upon this constitutional platform until they have torn away the last plank from under our feet. I desire to say here to-night that I believe we can win on the constitutional platform. But if we cannot win upon it, well, I shall be prepared to give way to better and stronger men, and it can never be said of us that by anything that we have done we have prevented better or abler men than ourselves from dealing with the future of our race.'

AT NAVAN

March 21st [1891]

'Now I come to the time in Committee Room No. 15, when your gallant Members stood united by my side against English dictation and intimidation. Mahony and Shiel[35] were there ... We were surrounded by a host of enemies. I could not attempt if I had the eloquence of Demosthenes and the ability of Cicero to depict to you the extraordinary system that was carried on throughout the House of Commons and throughout London for the purpose of sapping the courage and independence of my colleagues. I could not describe it to you. But there we were thirty against six hundred, and we beat them. We drove the false majority of the seceders out before us from Committee Room No 15, and we showed what raw troops they were when they allowed the minority to drive them out. We will drive them out of Ireland yet before we are done, and out of the House of Commons.'

AT THE BANQUET IN NAVAN

'We veterans have not broken our knees yet, and we have not got shortwinded, and we are able to stay as well as we used to, and I am confident that the Irish people who have watched our performance for sixteen years, are satisfied with the work we have done. I have got this to say that no leader either in the camp or field was ever rejected by a nation for the alleged cause for which you are ordered to reject me.'

AT MAYNOOTH

March 15th [1891]

'They (the seceders) have no platform to stand on except a platform of falsehood, in fact if it were not pitiable it would be ludicrous to see the attempts that they make to mislead the good sense of the people . . . But their day has come, and they have been found out, and Ireland will not long put up with them.'

AT MOYVALLEY

'The young men of Ireland will be the future of Ireland, and the cause that has the young men on its side is sure to win.'

AT ATHLONE

'I am going to tell you this that the Bishops did not help us to found either the Land League or the Irish National League, and both these organizations succeeded, and became great organizations, which made their mark upon the history of Ireland, and upon the history of the world . . . I am confident that Athlone and Westmeath will strike their blow when the time comes for an independent Irish Parliament, free from the dictation of any English party or statesman, with power to protect and conserve the interests of every class in our nation, and above all the power to keep these rights when we have won them.'

AT GALWAY

'You are not going to turn your backs upon your pledges and to eat your words while they are still fresh from your mouths like those recreant members for the city and county of Galway. No; you men of Galway know the road you take, and know your own minds, and knowing it you will stand by it. We are now again, as we were in 1880, at the commencement of a new and a great struggle, and I am as confident as I was then that the result of the fight will be of equal benefit to Ireland. Was it not better, was it not fortunate, that the rotten limbs in our movement were discovered in time. Was it not happy for Ireland, that the insidious attempts of whiggery to put the fetters round your limbs once more were made plain and evident to every comprehension before they enmeshed you . . . You have taken the conspiracy by the throat and you will strangle it in your strong grasp, and this time it will not be a scotched snake but a dead one. It was very well, I am sure it was very well, that we had the opportunity of clearing the decks, and of seeing who was true to Ireland, and who was merely trading and attempting to batten on the splendid national spirit of the country.'

AT A BANQUET IN CORK

March 17th [1891]

'. . . There is one thing, ladies and gentlemen, that you may be assured of, you will not get any English party to help you and to save you unless you first show that you are sufficiently powerful to help and to save yourselves, and above all things you will not get any English party to help or to stand by you if you run cringing to them, or allow your representatives to cringe to them, and to attempt to think that you can do nothing without the alliance of the Liberal party . . . We are happy to reflect in our faint and feeble way so long as we are sent to Westminster the spirit of the people that has sent us, and it is a bad chance for Ireland, a bad look out for our nation and our country, should ever the recreancy which has been unhappily shown by a number of our Irish representatives be successful . . . With the youth of Ireland upon my side, with all that is patriotic and brave upon my side, whenever it is necessary for me to come amongst you once more to ask again for your suffrages and your confidence, I shall come as I did in 1880, believing that you will again stand by me and rally to my side; and that the sentiment and judgment and knowledge of rebel Cork will be friendly and support me as it did then.'

AT DROGHEDA

March 22nd [1891]

'And if I consult my own wishes in the future, when Ireland has a right to send her representatives to a Legislature in College Green, I shall certainly choose some other position than that of a paid officer to the Crown, even subject to the wishes of my own countrymen. This crisis never would have come about if the Irish Parliamentary party represented the feelings of all that is courageous and determined in Irish politics. But they were carried away by the vortex of sham hypocritical intimidation, and they yielded to pressure not from their own countrymen but to pressure from Englishmen, and in so doing they showed themselves unworthy of the proud position of members of the Irish Parliamentary party . . . Once Ireland cringes to England, and proclaims that Ireland is helpless without English help, the future of our action is ruined and undone . . . I am satisfied that the public opinion of Ireland is on my side, and that we shall come triumphant out of this bitter and desperate struggle, which must now be fought out to the bitter end until one side or the other wins; and it is certain as the day succeeds the night that unless Ireland stands true to herself and superior to the influences that are being used against her, that our chance as a united Ireland will never be realised, and that the future of Home Rule, instead of being postponed for a few years, as our enemies claim will be the case, unless you prove traitors or recreants, will be postponed until the youngest man amongst us will grow grey, and descend to his grave recanting this treason to the Irish people . . . We have never won anything by humble requests and petitions, we never won anything by exhibiting ourselves as mendicants and as beseechers for English charity, or as reliant upon English good faith.'

DURING SLIGO ELECTION CONTEST [36]

'Fight this out, and bring these miserable seceders into their proper places, and when you have once more got a united Ireland back again press forward against the common foe, until you have once more compelled the English party to concede a full measure of Legislative independence.'

FROM MANIFESTO TO THE IRISH IN GREAT BRITAIN

'It was my policy to make English parties subservient to Irish interests. That policy was successful. It bore fruit in the Land Act of 1881, in the Arrears Act of 1882, in the Land Purchase Bill of 1885, in the Home Rule Bill of 1886, and in the Amended Land Act, 1887. We were united and strong, and both English parties were ready to treat with us. We wrung concessions from both; but weakened now by the desertion, in a moment of panic, of raw recruits led by terrified captains, it is sought to make our organization subservient to English interests – to make it the mere instrument of English parties. That policy, if successful, will bear fruit too. It will end in disorganization and utter ruin.'

AT KILDARE

May 3rd [1891]

'. . . And when now false prophets have arisen to tell you that Ireland's safety can only be obtained by an alliance with one particular English party, by abandoning our independence at the bid of one particular English statesman, my reply is, that that was not the doctrine which you accepted from me in 1880, and that is not the way or the method by which you won everything you have gained; that was not the way by which you compelled the attention of both English parties to the legitimate aspirations of Ireland, and that will not be the way in which Ireland will ever gain concessions of her right or respect for herself . . . I do not care what Government gives Ireland a concession. I am sorry to say that the seceders, in their handling of this question of the evicted tenants, have shown from first to last an utter want of political knowledge and capacity, and an utter and most extraordinary unscrupulousness of character.'

AT BELFAST

May 22nd [1891]

'Why, then, when we have refused persistently, and steadfastly refused through these sixteen years, to acknowledge the right of an English political party or English leader to dictate to us or call upon us to recognise their public opinion, or seeing that it was not by their resolution that we have secured the position that Ireland has held, and will still continue to hold if she be only true to herself – why, then, should we turn our back upon those lessons of the past, or these proofs that have been so repeatedly given by the march of these events, that we would be justified in belying the principles on which we took our stand during these long years . . . I decline to surrender any single safeguard for Ireland until we have seen what Mr Gladstone is able and willing to do for us . . . Sir William Harcourt has given us his definition of Home Rule. He says that it is to be such a Home Rule as the English party shall be able to give us – that we may either take it or leave it . . . Parliamentary action is a weapon which requires to be most carefully watched. It may deceive those who rely on it. It has deceived our people before . . . I say that it will be the fault of the Irish people, and of nobody else, if they allow themselves to be deceived in giving their votes at the next general election on behalf of men who have shown by their cowardice, recreancy, and vacillation that they are unfit to exercise on your behalf the power and the responsible position of the nation's representatives . . . I have a very shrewd impression in my mind that if the seceders succeed in putting down all independent opinion in the Irish people, that they will get about as good a Home Rule Bill as Lord Salisbury would be perfectly willing to give at any time, about as good a Home Rule Bill as our Orange friends in Belfast would be willing to accept – a Home Rule Bill which would leave the administration of justice, the maintenance of law and order, the control of the constabulary, the appointment of the magistrates and judges, and the settlement of the land question, all in the hands of the Imperial Legislature . . . We will never get the power to persuade, or induce, or stiffen up any English Ministry again if Ireland loses her independence or allows her Parliamentary Party to lose their independence.'

AT WICKLOW

May 31st [1891]

'I will only say of his Grace (of Cashel), that while I believe his Grace is a most excellent Archbishop, I don't believe him to be a good political leader.'

AT BERMONDSEY, LONDON

June 17th [1891]

'I say another thing, that if Ireland does surrender the independence of the majority of her members, that you will never get from Mr Gladstone or from any statesman any concession. You will never send the House of Lords about their business on an Irish question, you may on an English one. We know that we are going to win, and that we intend to fight this out in England and Ireland till we have won, and we shall submit this question for decision to constituency after constituency till we get the opportunity at the next general election of asking the whole of Ireland to say aye or no.'

AT BALBRIGGAN

June 21st [1891]

'But Mr Gladstone did not do any of these things which he might have done if he pleased, but he interfered in a question belonging solely to the Irish party, and in so doing he showed that he had not the slightest appreciation of the position which Irish members took up sixteen years ago when we formed an Independent Irish party – that he had not the slightest knowledge of the strength of the forces upon which Irish members depended for their existence, and upon which the unity and strength of Ireland depends, and must always depend, so that in leaving the seceders with their new leader, Mr Gladstone, I may tell you that they left undone those things they ought to have done, and did those things they ought not to have done . . .Yet, if we once obtained a Parliament called a Parliament, with some of its powers, and retained our own independence as a Parliamentary party, and the independence of our country, all things would come afterwards.'

AT CARLOW

June 29th [1891]

'I shall see that no compromise be made between an Irish renegade party and an English party which will prevent the Irish people from obtaining the legitimate results of the great advances we have made in those years past. I tell you whatever counsels of timidity and cowardice may be preached to you by the seceders, do not be afraid to express your opinion on this question . . . And were it not for the desertion and panic of the seceders, they would win from the British Parliament a full measure of those just claims which the party had been formed to secure. Retaining our independence we can gain all things, it is a question of time and of exertion for the future, but unquestionably by retaining our independence, and insisting upon the independence of our members at Westminster, we can gain all things – and we have gained much in this way'

AFTER RESULT OF CARLOW ELECTION WAS MADE KNOWN [37]

'If they should happen to be beaten at the next general election, they would form a solid rallying square with the 1,500 good men who voted for Ireland's nationhood in the County Carlow, of the 2,500 heroes who voted for the same cause in North Sligo, and of the 1,400 voters in North Kilkenny, who stood by the flag of Irish independence, for

> Freedom's battle once begun –
> Bequeathed by bleeding sire to son –
> Though baffled oft' is always won.'

AT LIMERICK

May 23rd [1891]

'A struggle has been commenced which will have to be fought out to the end.'

AT LIMERICK

May 24th [1891]

'I was confident from the first moment when these troubles commenced that it was my duty to do one of two things either to fight the battle out to the end or to obtain such securities from the

English party which asked Ireland to surrender her independence and freedom of judgment, and independence should be attended with as little ill and mischief to our country as possible . . . If I were driven from my position as leader of the nation, I should still continue to battle on behalf of independent Ireland, of freedom of action and thought for my countrymen. As citizen of Ireland, it would be still my duty to go on with this fight. I tell you, fellow-countrymen, that once you allow your members to break the ranks, to lose their independence, to take their orders from an English political party or English statesman, then you may bid good bye to hopes of benefits and reform for Ireland by political action and that powerful constitutional weapon which I forged for you, and which I put into your hands and taught you to use with advantage to yourselves, will break and be shattered in your hands, and that proud position which Ireland has attained will be lost for ever if our countrymen once forget the teachings of history and are forgetful of the means by which they have won their proud position of strength and independence.'

AT INCHICORE, CO. DUBLIN

June 8th [1891]

'Ireland has been alternately threatened by seceders, by Liberals, and by English Governments, that unless they lay aside their independence Irish liberty will be lost. I stand here to-day to declare to you, as always, that Irish liberties depend upon Irish public spirit and Irish feeling of independence. I do not agree that Ireland's future depends upon any English political party, or upon any English statesman, I do not believe a word of it. His Grace the Archbishop of Cashel said the other day that Home Rule was dead and buried. If it were possible to kill Home Rule it would have been killed by the action of the seceders and by the action of his Grace.

But it is not possible to kill it so long as you hold fast by the principles which produced it.'

AT NEWCASTLE–ON–TYNE

July 19th [1891]

'... An independent policy is always a rotten policy in the mind of a rotten individual... Amongst the last words which the respected member for this town spoke to me was an expression of apprehension that Ireland would be profoundly disappointed and discontented when it was found on the coming of the Liberals into office how very little the Liberals would be able to do for them.'

AT THURLES

August 2nd [1891]

{Messrs. Dillon and O'Brien, who had gone into Galway Gaol without any definite declaration of their opinions on the leadership question, lost not a moment after their release to proclaim themselves supporters of Mr Timothy Healy. From the prison gates they were taken in the Bishop's carriage to the episcopal residence, and there entertained.[38] An hour afterwards they proceeded to denounce Mr Parnell in the orthodox seceders' fashion.}

'I hoped and believed from my conversations with him (William O'Brien), prior to his going to jail, at Boulogne and elsewhere, that he would have come out a neutral and not an enemy, and that I might at least have been able to regard him as amongst the number of my old friends. It appears that this is no longer possible, and that no meeting between us now could be of much avail. I regret that it should have been so, more especially, I say, in his case, because, as I have more than once said, he is a man whose friendship and support in my public life I have always specially valued. It is a terrible and a great blow to me personally to be severed from such a friend, but if it needs must be so, it must be so . . . I fear that the time has now come for the Irish people to choose sides irrevocably, whether they will lay down their arms unconditionally, whether they will decide to instruct their representatives in the coming Parliament to make the lasting treaty of peace with England – a treaty from which the people of Ireland cannot draw back once made – with the knowledge of what the conditions of that treaty of peace is going to be. Mr Dillon says that he will draw the sword again if the Liberal Party deceive him. But what if he has no sword to draw. Who have been his armies in the past in fighting English powers? What has been his sword? Have these armies consisted of the clergy and bishops of Ireland? (No, no). No; they have been made up of the men who have been on my side in this struggle, and having handed these, his ancient allies, over to this system of intimidation and of persecution which is sought to be brought against them in every quarter in Ireland, how can he when he discovers the futility of English promises call back these vanished hosts. Mr Dillon says now that he is in favour of unity, and that it was by unity and strict discipline that we attained our successes in the past. I will tell you, fellow-countrymen, that it was by something greater and stronger than unity and discipline that we obtained this success. It was because we were independent . . . Believe me, my friends, Ireland will not have to regret that so many of her sons are not afraid of being on the side of the minority . . . Whether we are beaten at the general election or whether we win, we shall live to win. It is no longer a question of leadership. It is question whether our country is worthy of being a nation.'

AT THE NATIONAL CLUB

Same date [August 2nd 1891]

'The men of Tipperary showed to-day just as the men of Dublin show to-night, that they are, as they have always been, independent Irishmen, and that no matter how great the position and services of men who seek to lead them astray, they know how to follow the instincts, the unfailing instincts of their own heart, and their own judgment. You have been sought to be intimidated by every device which the ingenuity of man could devise; you have been sought to be drawn away from the pole star of Irish Nationality; but there exists throughout the length and breadth of Ireland a body of independent Irishmen, who, in the face of every intimidation, will see that nothing shall cloud the light which shines upon the National path, and that your faith is the faith which guided the courage of Robert Emmet and of Lord Edward Fitzgerald – a burning desire to give Ireland her legitimate freedom, and to give our country a chance to prosper and succeed in the race of nationhood, and determined that you will follow no English party, no English directions until you have tested the length and the breadth of these English promises. You know well that Ireland will lose nothing by your independence. Mr Dillon and Mr O'Brien say that they too will draw the sword, and that they will draw it at the end of a twelvemonth if English promises prove faithless. But how are they going to draw the sword if they have thrown it away, if they have handed it over to the captain of the other ship. Are they sure that he will give them their sword back again when they want to use it? And where is their army gone? What forces are they going to fight with when twelve months are over? You, men, formerly constituted their army; upon you, men, and such men as you, throughout Ireland, they depended for their fame, position and strength. It has been one of the bitterest pains of my life that Mr

O'Brien has separated himself from me. I will not say that he has separated himself from me because I did not ask him to support me. It has been to me a bitter pain that he should have joined the ranks of my enemies. I have always looked up to him, and fondly regarded him as my friend. I had hoped before he came out from Galway prison that he might have pondered a while, and that his attitude might be different, but I leave his action with this reflection, and this reflection only, that in the words of the poet –

> Of all the words of tongue and pen,
> The saddest are – "It might have been"[39]

William O'Brien might have been my colleague in the future. He might have joined with me in welcoming back the freedom of Ireland. He might have helped me after a time in securing for our people independent expression of their opinions, in tranquilising the fears of the Protestant section of our fellow-countrymen, and in showing the nations that, while she desires freedom above all things, Ireland also desires to use that freedom with toleration to all. His genius, his great courage, his indomitable resolution, would be invaluable for these objects and great ends and aims. But my poor friend has taken another path; he has for a time at least, I fear, turned his back upon his old friends who never turned their backs upon him. He appears to have forgotten that Ireland's strength comes from the independent ones of her children, and from no other source. I trust that the step is not irremediable or irrevocable. I had hoped that he would have been, as I once called him, the Strongbow of Irish Nationality by the side of all that is independent, true, and brave among his fellow-countrymen in the assertion of the National right to the freedom of our country.'

AT DUBLIN EN ROUTE TO KELLS

August 16th [1891]

'Whoever is going to retire you will not, and whether the fight is going to be a long one or a short one we will be there at the end, and we are confident that we will be on the winning side.'

AT KELLS

August 16th [1891]

'It will be easier for a camel to go through the eye of a needle than for Mr Gladstone or Mr Morley to restore any single evicted tenant to his holding. Mr Dillon knows this well, and it is shameful for him to seek to continue a hopeless struggle at New Tipperary and other estates; to condemn men, their wives and families, to lose everything they possessed, to lose their homes and their futures merely for the purpose of obtaining an additional weapon against me in this struggle . . . I am glad to be free of this English alliance – free as the air of my own Wicklow mountains. The responsibility, a heavy one, has been taken off my shoulders, and I will not reassume it. I am glad to be by the side of the freemen and liberty-loving men of Ireland, and I know that those men, whether they are few or many in number, and I know that they are many, will stand shoulder to shoulder, will refuse to surrender their independence to an English political party, will decline to go under the other yoke in Ireland, until they are satisfied that the future of Ireland is safe, and that they can safely give up the constitutional weapons which they have now firmly grasped in their brave stalwart hands.'

AT COMMERCIAL BRANCH, I. N. L.

August 28th [1891]

'The movement and the battle which are before us will be a long one, and undoubtedly a most difficult one. But whether it takes one year or whether it takes several years – and it will, probably, take several years – it can end only in one way. It can end only in the justification of the Nationalists of Ireland who, in the face of every difficulty and discredit sought to be thrown upon them, have taken their stand on the side of Irish independence at the present juncture. It is beyond question true that they will find their justification in the march of events, and that though the fight may undoubtedly be a difficult one, it will be a winning one for them and for you. I feel as confident as I am of my existence that the Nationalists of Ireland will be justified by the results of this fight and this battle, and that the day will come when our countrymen, unanimously at home and abroad, though their minds may be for a time clouded with doubts, will see and recognise that you have been justified by the result . . . And I think that the conduct of Mr Gray, as contrasted with the other members of the staff of the *Freeman*, offers us an example of everything that is to be avoided in journalism and in public life.'

AT AMNESTY MEETING HELD IN PHOENIX PARK

August 30th [1891]

'I always think that mere politicians, mere members of Parliament, ought to feel ashamed of themselves when they are permitted to stand upon an amnesty platform and to plead on behalf of men who have shown by those many years of suffering how pure and how good was their love for Ireland. And we should be stimulated, every one of us, whether we be members of Parliament or whether we be others working at home, we should be stimulated by the reflections which crowd upon our minds at the utterance of this word amnesty, to renewed exertions, that we shall leave nothing undone until these hard and cruel prison doors have been opened, and until these patriotic Irishmen once more see the light of a free heaven . . . Ireland owes much – has owed much at all times – perhaps still will have to owe much to her political prisoners. I have often felt in my own heart, and I have sometimes said – perhaps not as often as I should have said it, but still not to-day, by many times for the first time – that Ireland is much indebted to her political prisoners. Had it not been for them, for the spirit which Ireland's political prisoners and Ireland's martyrs have at all times kept alive in the Irish heart, we should not to-day have an Irish nation to struggle for . . . Ireland may be confident of her future to-day; she may turn her back on her old friends, but there is one thing she will never do, she will never forget the cause of amnesty.'

AT WESTPORT

September 6th [1891]

'Some of the seceders – the great majority of them – have only changed twice. But as regards the two gentlemen of whom I desire to speak with every respect – Messrs. Dillon and O'Brien – they have changed four times. Let us, let you, the Nationalists of the West, take care that in this struggle, surrounded as it is by so many pitfalls and temptations, surrounded as the question of constitutional and Parliamentary exertion, and all alliances with an English party or parties undoubtedly is with so many dangers of backsliding and of treachery, you will take care, I am confident, that you will do your part that the National claim, the National position, and the National independence of our country shall not be tampered with by any of them, but that it shall be preserved sacred as it always has been in these historic plains, and that the men of Mayo will be as true as they were in 1798, when perfectly sure of defeat, and of loss of their own lives and of their own property, they faced that defeat and faced that death. So you are to-day facing a present defeat with the knowledge that time will justify us, and that the majority of our people will admit that we were right when we decided to preserve above all things the independent position of our country and our representatives at this time of crisis and of struggle. I am confident of this, there is enough independent strength in Ireland of sterling Irish Nationalists to declare that they are not afraid of being in a minority as long as may be necessary in order that they may secure the independence and the nationhood of our race . . . Ireland's party must be separate and independent. She cannot mingle without being faithless to her trust; she cannot mingle the rank and file of her party with the rank and file of an English party. She cannot take her orders from these English parties or their leaders. What is the history of this question from first to last? Every move has been dictated to the seceders by the English Press and by the members of an English party. It has not been Ireland's wish, Ireland's idea, Ireland's motive power, but it has been the orders, the wishes, the motive power of the English, their parties, their clubs, and their leaders.'

AT LISTOWEL

September 13th [1891]

'But what I conceive we are striving for is this – they say that because they happen to constitute the majority of the Irish members that therefore they are entitled to bind the minority not only of the Irish members, but also of the Irish people – to compel the minority to obey their orders. That might have been so had it happened that these orders were not given by Mr Gladstone. But we strive not for leadership. We strive to preserve our own independence and the independence of our country, which these men say we are to give up to them because they contend they are in the majority. What would you say to the consistency and judgment of a man who announces to-day that it was a ridiculous thing to go to Mr Gladstone and ask for pledges, and who, six or seven months before at Boulogne, was a party to an arrangement by which Mr Gladstone was asked for pledges. He (Mr Dillon) was quite willing to do a ridiculous thing, and agree to a ridiculous thing, so long as he saw any chance of keeping me out of public life, and getting me to retire. A very curious thing in connection with these Boulogne negotiations, when talking of judgment and common-sense – I will not say statesmanship – that the only portions of them that Mr O'Brien begged me not to publish, in case during his imprisonment I found it necessary to publish any portion of them, were the proposals composed by Mr O'Brien, with the help of Mr Dillon, in America, before he left, accepted by Mr McCarthy and Mr Sexton when he arrived in France, and actually proposed to me as a solution of the question, and which I found so absurd and ridiculous, and so traitorous to the Liberal allies of these men that they were obliged to admit that they were utterly untenable and unsuitable. Mr O'Brien can publish these proposals if he chooses, and also the counter proposals I made afterwards if he wishes, not because I think that the counter proposals that I made were suitable or sufficient, and had not many faults in them, but because it was the best thing that I could advise at the moment for the purpose of satisfying the desire which existed in the country, that the peril in some way or other should be got over, and a settlement of this dispute should be arrived at.

'If I were dead and gone to-morrow, the men who are fighting against English influence in Irish public life would fight on still; they would still be Independent Nationalists;

they would still believe in the future of Ireland a Nation; and they would still protest that it was not by taking orders from an English Minister that Ireland's future could be saved, protected, or secured.[40]

'I will not be a party to setting up the power of the Liberal party which it is sought to put over us in England, and the power of another sort sought to be put over us in Ireland. I trust that the coming Local Government Bill of the present Government may contain provisions which will be of the utmost good to the labouring classes of the country. If it does not contain these provisions, it will be our duty to leave no stone unturned to see that before that measure leaves the House of Commons it shall have such provisions added to it, and certainly, if we can manage it in any way we will put into that measure provisions that will enable many a poor labouring man who has to emigrate at the present moment to stay at home, to bring up his family at home, and be one of the future mainstays and strength of Ireland a nation. Now, fellow-countrymen, of amnesty. I should have gladly welcomed the presence of Mr O'Brien and Mr Dillon on the platform at the Phoenix Park. But if they did not like to come on our platform, let them get one of their own and advocate the cause of the captives from that platform. They cannot consistently maintain the attitude of silence, and of neutrality upon this question, merely because their new leader, Sir William Harcourt, thinks political prisoners have not been sufficiently punished for the offences they committed so many years ago. They must shake themselves loose from their English allies upon this question if they are going to maintain a single shred of their title as Irish Nationalists . . . It is idle, then, to seek to persuade you that this is merely a question of leadership. It is a question of a grave difference of opinion as to the means by which the future of our country can be secured. I agree to the fullest extent that Ireland's cause is independent of any man. Ireland's cause would live as it has lived, and we believe will live, despite the efforts of traitorous and cowardly seceders; and if the seceders swept us all out of public life to-morrow, Ireland's cause would still survive. This struggle is not continued for the purpose of supporting the claim of any man, but for the purpose of declaring that the conduct of the chosen representatives of Ireland who elected their leader on the morning of one day, and on the afternoon of that same day, because an English leader ordered them to do so, reversed their decision, was conduct unworthy of Irish Nationalists, and most unworthy of men who put themselves forward as representatives of the Irish nation . . . What we are fighting for? We assert to-day in this town of Listowel what we asserted in 1885 and the years before it, that no man has a right to fix the boundary of a nation – that no man has a right to limit the aspirations of our people.'

HIS LAST SPEECH AT CREGGS

September 27th [1891]

{Though suffering greatly from an acute attack of rheumatism, he went to Creggs against the advice of his doctor; and in the course of this, his last speech, referring to his own health, he said:}

'If I had taken the advice of my doctor I should have gone to bed when I arrived in Dublin the night previous, but if I had done that my enemies would be throwing up their hats, and announcing that I was dead before I was buried . . .

'I have never kept the question of leadership up to the front, and I have never abandoned any question of leadership. My desire in setting out was not to lead any people, but to put our people in the path to lead themselves, so that they would be able to choose their own leader; and when that day comes that a self-governed Ireland is able to guard and cherish her own honour and her own destiny, then I promise these men who to-day talk about facts and the will of the Irish nation, that I will poll throughout all Ireland man for man, and more than man for man, of independent Irishmen in protest against this doctrine which is now preached to us that the strong arm of the Liberal party is supreme for the purpose of gaining freedom for Ireland. We are told in these days that the voice of the Church is the voice of God, and that, therefore, it must be obeyed in politics. That was not the condition upon which I entered public life sixteen years ago. It never struck me at any time during these sixteen years that the Irish clergy were particularly skilful politicians . . .

{Referring to the Boulogne negotiations.}

. . . The great fundamental differences will be apparent when Mr O'Brien publishes these proposals from himself, my counter proposals, and my amendment to those Liberal proposals. It will then be seen that I was not fighting for my hand and for my own leadership, but that I was striving to secure as well as I could, in my hampered condition, some strength for Ireland to deal with her own future when the Liberals come into power . . . I tell you, men of Roscommon and of Galway, that if the day ever comes when your Irish members come to believe that they cannot do anything without leaning upon the strong arm of the Liberal party, it is a good strong kick your Irish members will get from behind from the Liberal party . . . I gave up none of my independence or that of my colleagues to Mr Gladstone when I came out of Kilmainham to obtain these great benefits (the Arrears Act), and the truth of that was shown by our subsequent years of fight against Mr Gladstone and the Liberal party until we threw them out of power in '85 without Mr Dillon's assistance, he having retired from his country to America, despairing of the future of Ireland . . . We shall continue this fight. We fight not for faction, but for freedom . . . I know that you look to Ireland's future as a nation if we gain it. We may not be able to gain it, but if not it will be left for those who come after us to win; but we will do our best.'

{Mr Parnell's last letter to his mother, in answer to her complaint of how some of the American papers had written of his treatment of her:}

'I am weary, dear mother, of these troubles, weary unto death; but it is all in a good cause. With health, and the assistance of my friends, I am confident of the result. The statements my enemies have so often made, regarding my relations with you, are on a par with the endless calumnies they shoot upon me from behind every bush. Let them pass. They will die of their own venom. It would, indeed, be dignifying them to notice their existence.'

> Bury him standing, as kings of old –
> He will not rest,
> Though on Ireland's breast
> He lieth cold
> He is not dead; he cannot die
> Remember it, brothers, early and late,
> Our king is buried, but not his heart,
> For we of his life have kept our part,
> We are his love, and we are his hate;
> His sword are we, he strikes the blow,
> He leads us onward to strike the foe;
> His voice is our battle cry
> And our bugle call,
> From amongst the dead, where over all
> He standeth tall

HIS LAST WORDS: [41]

'ʒive my love to my colleaʒues
and to the ırısh people'

Editors' Notes

Introduction by Anna Parnell

1   From James Russell Lowell (1818–91), 'Stanzas on Freedom'.

Words of the Dead Chief

1   From Byron's play, *Marino Falierno*. The full quotation reads 'They never fail who die/In a *great* cause; the block may soak their gore;/Their heads may sodden in the sun; their limbs/ Be strung to castle gates and city walls/ But still their spirit walks abroad.' Marino Falierno, Doge of Venice, was executed in 1355.

2   This should be 12 April 1875.

3   An explosion at Clerkenwell prison, London, on 13 December 1869 in an attempt to free two Fenian prisoners caused several deaths and injuries.

4   A shot into a police van in Manchester on 18 September 1867 during the rescue of two Fenian prisoners killed Sergeant Brett and resulted in the execution of the 'Manchester Martyrs'.

5   Sir Stafford Northcote.

6   Gaythorne Hardy.

7   Sergeant McCarthy – a former soldier, convicted of Fenian sympathies; suffering a heart condition yet made do hard labour; released with Michael Davitt; died of a heart attack while attending a breakfast hosted by Parnell.

8   William Habron wrongly sentenced to death for the murder of a policeman. Because of his age, the sentence was commuted to penal servitude for life. Three years later a notorious criminal confessed to the murder and Habron was pardoned.

9   Gaythorne Hardy, W. H. Smith and R. A. Cross respectively.

10 This meeting to which Parnell travelled by night train directly after the Rotunda meeting was held on 22 November.

11 Parnell visited the United States in 1876 with an official address on the occasion of the centenary of American independence.

12 On 21 February Parnell received the freedom of the city of Chicago and addressed an assembly of about ten thousand – the largest meeting of the mission.

13 Parnell probably said 'break'.

14 He was elected chairman of the party on 17 May 1880.

15 William Edward Forster.

16 Charles Bradlaugh, atheist and free-thinker was elected MP for Northampton in 1880 but expelled and imprisoned for a time when he refused to take a religious oath. His seat was declared vacant but he was re-elected on four successive occasions. To the surprise and annoyance of many of his colleagues, Parnell supported Bradlaugh in 1880. However, in 1883, he reversed his position.

17 These lines are from 'The Ballad of Richard Burnell' by English Quaker poet Mary Howitt (1799–1888). Howitt's most famous poem was 'The Spider and the Fly'.

18 Probably Rt Hon. David Plunket, Solicitor General for Ireland (1875–7), later Baron Rathmore of Shanganagh.

19 Joseph P. Ronayne, the late Home Rule MP for Cork and proponent of obstruction in the House of Commons.

20 Carey, a leading member of the Invincibles involved in the Phoenix Park murders of Cavendish, the Chief Secretary, and Burke, the Under Secretary, turned informer and his evidence led to the execution of five of his colleagues. He was shot dead on board a ship off Cape Town by a former colleague in the Invincibles.

21 Captain Plunkett was the Divisional Magistrate. Later, in March 1887 when a riotous assembly was expected at Youghal, he instructed the local police inspector: 'If necessary do not hesitate to shoot them.'

22 Myles Joyce was one of three hanged for the murder of a family of five at Maamtrasna, Co. Galway, in August 1882, though the other two before their execution declared him innocent.

23 Parnell used the occasion of his visit to Plymouth to praise the Plymouth Brethren. The Brethren grew rapidly from the late 1820s and attracted significant support in Wicklow. Lady Powerscourt, Parnell's aunt Catherine, her

husband George Vicesimus Wigram and her cousin John Parnell (Lord Congleton), all converted to the Brethren.

24 The earl of Carnarvon, Tory Lord Lieutenant, had earlier been involved in secret discussions with Parnell about an Irish settlement but Lord Salisbury abruptly announced a return to coercion.

25 Sir Michael Hicks Beach.

26 Notorious evictions and deliberate destruction of several cottages at Glenbeigh, County Kerry, took place on the estate of the Hon. Rowland Winn in January 1887. Major General Buller, the Special Commissioner in Ireland, had sought in vain for an abatement of the tenants' rent.

27 Arthur Balfour.

28 Canon Keller PP of Youghal was imprisoned in 1887 for refusing to give evidence about the Plan of Campaign conducted by the tenants on the Ponsonby estate. Nationalist opinion was enraged. Archbishop Walsh of Dublin, MPs, aldermen and citizens accompanied the prisoner to the gates of Kilmainham.

29 Joseph Chamberlain MP for Birmingham left the Liberals on Gladstone's Home Rule Bill to become a Liberal Unionist.

30 Colonel Alfred Turner was Special Commissioner of the RIC for counties Cork, Clare, Kerry and Limerick, 1886–92.

31 William O'Brien, MP for Cork North-east, editor of *United Ireland*, one of the leaders of the Plan of Campaign.

32 J. L. Carew, MP for Kildare North.

33 John Mandeville, a local farmer, with O'Brien he was charged with making inflammatory speeches while organising the Plan of Campaign on the Kingston estate. He died seven months after his release from custody as a result of his treatment in prison according to the verdict of the coroner's inquest.

34 John Dillon.

35 Pierce Mahony and Edward Shiel were the two MPs elected for Meath in the general election of 1886. They sided with Parnell in Committee Room 15.

36 The Sligo North election took place on 2 April 1891.

37 Polling in Carlow took place on 7 July 1891. The anti-Parnellite candidate, John Hammond, defeated the Parnellite, Andrew Kettle.

38 The Bishop of Galway was Francis MacCormack, suspected by English officials of supporting the Plan of Campaign leaders.

39 This is a quotation from 'Maud Muller', a poem by the American Quaker poet, John Greenleaf Whittier (1807–92). Born in Massachusetts, Whittier was a leading abolitionist.

40 This paragraph was printed in bold type in the original edition.

41 When Parnell's body lay in state in the City Hall on the day of his funeral, these so-called last words were emblazoned on the walls. Dr Jowers, Parnell's physician was cited as the source of this last message. However, his wife Katharine reported Parnell's last words as being 'Kiss me, sweet wifie, and I will try to sleep a little.'